history's children

ANNA CLARK is an Australian Postdoctoral Fellow in history education at Monash University. She is the author of *Teaching the Nation* (Melbourne University Press, 2006); *Convicted!* (Hardie Grant Egmont, 2005), which was listed as a 2006 Children's Book Council of Australia Notable Book; and *The History Wars* with Stuart Macintyre (Melbourne University Press, 2003), winner of the NSW Premier's Prize for Australian History and the Queensland Premier's Prize for Best Literary or Media Work Advancing Public Debate.

history's children

HISTORY WARS IN THE CLASSROOM

ANNA CLARK

NEW SOUTH

A New South book

Published by
University of New South Wales Press Ltd
University of New South Wales
Sydney NSW 2052
AUSTRALIA
www.unswpress.com.au

© Anna Clark 2008
First published 2008

This book is copyright. Apart from any fair dealing for the purpose of private study, research, criticism or review, as permitted under the Copyright Act, no part may be reproduced by any process without written permission. Inquiries should be addressed to the publisher.

National Library of Australia
Cataloguing-in-Publication entry

> Clark, Anna, 1978– .
> History's children: history wars in the classroom.
>
> Includes index.
> ISBN 978 086840 863 7 (pbk.).
>
> 1. Educational surveys - Australia. 2. Australian students - Attitudes. 3. Australia - History - Study and teaching. 4. Australia - Historiography. I. Title.
>
> 907.20994

Design Josephine Pajor-Markus
Cover Boheem Design
Printer Ligare

This book is printed on paper using fibre supplied from plantation or sustainably managed forests.

Contents

Acknowledgments	*vii*
Introduction	*1*
1 The 'Edmund Barton syndrome'	*20*
2 The allure of Anzac	*43*
3 1788 and all that	*64*
4 A national curriculum	*89*
5 History in the classroom	*112*
Conclusion	*140*
Further reading	*146*
Notes	*155*
Index	*174*

For my history teachers

Acknowledgments

There are many people I have to thank, and without whom this book could not have been completed.

First, to the schools and departments I visited: while history teaching continues to generate considerable public and political pressure, perspectives from the classroom itself have been notably absent from these debates. I am most grateful to the thirty-five principals from around Australia who let me visit their schools, the teachers and students who gave their time to speak with me, the group of student teachers at the University of Sydney, and the curriculum officials and department of education representatives who generously offered their opinions in their interviews. Their voices, thoughts and experiences form the foundation of this book.

I am also indebted to friends and family who read various chapter drafts (in various states of disarray): Gabriel Abramowitz, Simon Booth, Tania Lewis, Sean Scalmer and Clare Wright each gave much-needed feedback and support during the project and cannot be thanked enough for their help. In particular, my mum Alison and brother Tom both read full drafts of the book – and I thank them for their kindness and knowledge (especially all things grammatical). It is a great luxury to have such understanding readers of your work.

This book presents some Australian material from a project that compares the study of history teaching in Australia and Canada. The project was funded by a Discovery Grant from the Australian Research Council, and an Australian Postdoctoral Fellowship gave me the time and financial support to conduct this research – an amazing opportunity for a young researcher. I was also fortunate to visit the Centre for the Study of Historical Consciousness at the University of British Columbia in order to present some of this Australian research, and begin to conduct some of the Canadian interviews. My thanks go to Professor Peter Seixas and all at the centre for being such generous hosts.

The realisation of the book was made possible thanks to the interest and encouragement of my editor, Phillipa McGuinness, who seemed to see the project better than I could. Her comments, along with the warm and engaged response from an anonymous reader, gave me much to work with. I greatly appreciate the time they, and all those at UNSW Press, have given to this book.

Lastly, to my project colleagues Tony Taylor, Carmel Young and Stuart Macintyre, who offered much-needed advice and support, and the freedom to pursue this research, thank you.

Introduction

> **Robert:** *I feel like in history Australian history is relevant but I get the feeling that all through high school there's this massive push to be a patriot and to be involved and to understand about Australia. But I think it's one of the most boring countries in the world, and I'd rather learn about America or China or something like that.*
>
> **Jeffrey:** *At least America had the Civil War.*
>
> Year 12 students, Catholic boys' school, Perth

History teaching

What is it about Australian history? Students dismiss the subject for being boring while politicians and concerned parents fret over children's lack of historical knowledge. Teachers struggle to get their kids interested in Australia's past while history wars rage in the media all around them. For a subject that's widely dismissed for not exciting much emotion in the classroom, Australian history doesn't suffer from anything of the kind when it comes to anxious public debate over its status in schools.

Research reports that reveal low levels of historical knowledge among schoolchildren are worrying reminders of young Australians' apparent lack of interest in their nation's past. In 1997 a national survey showed that only 18 per cent of those interviewed knew Edmund Barton was Australia's first prime minister, for example; and in a 2006 report on the state of civics and citizenship only 23 per cent of year 10 students knew Australia Day celebrated the arrival of the British in 1788.[1]

These sorts of figures frighten even prime ministers. In his speech to the National Press Club in Canberra on the eve of Australia Day in 2006, John Howard called for the restoration of Australian history teaching in 'our schools' and claimed that only a 'root and branch renewal' of the subject could foster a lasting attachment to the nation's past. 'In the end,' he said, 'young people are at risk of being disinherited from their community if that community lacks the courage and confidence to teach its history'.[2] The following day, Howard's speech was on the front page of the major dailies, ABC television's '7.30 Report' ran a story on history education in Australian schools, and editors began to fill their papers and online forums with contributions from teachers, historians and other concerned correspondents.[3]

It's hardly the first time history teaching has hit headlines in Australia. Significant national anniversaries such as Australia Day or Anzac Day trigger almost annual public discussions about the subject in schools. In 2004 it was Remembrance Day that prompted Neil Wilson in Melbourne's *Herald-Sun* to question young people's historical sensibilities. 'How many teens think about why we mark Remembrance Day? Or the meaning of the poppy?' he wondered. A week before Anzac Day in 2006 the Victorian Returned Services League publicly lamented that while the Anzac story had become more prominent in recent years, many young people didn't fully appreciate the sacrifices made by Australian soldiers in war.[4]

It's natural that these historical markers generate public interest in the past and debates about how that history will in turn be passed on to the next generation. National commemorations are powerful and popular reminders of Australia's identity and heritage, but they mean many things to many people. And the bigger the anniversary, it seems, the bigger the debate.

During the Bicentenary in 1988 there were heated exchanges about which story of Australia the anniversary represented and how it should be taught in schools. Education unions threatened to boycott any syllabus that didn't adequately acknowledge Indigenous perspectives, just as conservative commentators called for greater pride in Australia's past. Meanwhile, teachers were left with a balancing act to present these competing histories to their classes.[5]

Was it really the 'Celebration of the Nation' the slogans promised? I remember getting up at the crack of dawn to watch the re-enactment of the First Fleet sail into Sydney Harbour as a nine year old, oblivious to the historical contest playing out before us. The harbour was festooned with banners and boats, but there were also significant protests paying tribute to Indigenous survival since 1788. Kids around the country were given commemorative medallions of the first governor, Arthur

Phillip, but some controversially returned theirs to Prime Minister Bob Hawke. One Aboriginal student from Sydney's Vaucluse High told his school assembly that he couldn't 'accept a medal that celebrates what has happened to our families'.[6]

Australian history isn't any clearer today, and the sort of debate surrounding the Bicentenary in 1988 continues to play out over history sites around the country. The National Museum of Australia was the subject of a much-publicised inquiry in 2003 after accusations that its exhibits presented an overly negative and biased account of Australia's past. Historians also fought fierce and lengthy battles after Keith Windschuttle suggested a 'major academic deception' had exaggerated the extent of colonial violence against Aboriginal people for political gains.[7]

Such questions dominate the so-called 'history wars' – those politicised and polarising debates that have raged over history books, museum exhibits and public anniversaries. School history has been particularly fraught. In the 1990s the use of the word 'invasion' to describe European colonisation in some teaching resources and syllabuses sparked slanging matches in Queensland, New South Wales and Victoria over the representation of Australian history in schools; these disputes reverberate today.[8] According to Jenny Lawless, the Inspector for History at the New South Wales Board of Studies, the politics of teaching the subject are 'always a nightmare'. 'It's just the nature of history,' she says. 'I get probably ten times more ministerials, letters and emails challenging whatever we have in the history curriculum than any other subject.'[9] Such disputes show how contested teaching the nation's past has become in Australia, as educators, historians and politicians find themselves increasingly entangled in an anxious public debate.

So the paradox persists: while kids continue to reject Australian history for being too boring, the subject seems more fraught than ever. The history wars have generated unprecedented coverage and interest in the past, but that doesn't appear to have translated into the classroom. Instead, research has revealed alarmingly low levels of knowledge about Australia's history, raising fears that a whole generation of students are completely out of touch with their nation's past – if they don't know the name of Australia's first prime minister, *what else* don't they know?

The blame has been laid on most areas of the education system: kids aren't interested, teachers aren't teaching it, and curriculum bodies aren't doing enough to promote Australian history in schools. Accusations from educationists, historians and sections of the media have been raised that history is being lost within catch-all subjects such as Studies of Society and Environment (or SOSE). They argue that students don't know their own history simply because it's not being taught.[10]

Should history be a stand-alone subject in schools, or is the traditional discipline approach no longer relevant today? In the 1990s every state and territory except New South Wales agreed to teach history through SOSE up to year 10. The move tried to bring greater coherence across all the subject areas between different education systems. But now, amidst this growing concern that historical understanding has been compromised, state and territory governments have reasserted the discipline approach in schools.[11]

Then there's the issue of Australian history in particular. Currently, each education system has its own approach to the subject, ranging from the mandatory Australian history syllabus taught in years 9 and 10 in New South Wales to the Queensland model, where there are no prescriptions of historical content whatsoever.[12] Perhaps it's appropriate in a country so far-flung as ours to have a regionalised approach to teaching national history. Many teachers and curriculum designers insist it's the only way that the individual needs of teachers and students can be accommodated. Others, including both major federal political parties, are equally adamant that all students should learn a consistent Australian story as part of their compulsory education.

It's the level of engagement that makes this discussion so interesting. Teachers have an obvious investment in Australian history education, and history teachers' associations have been particularly active to defend the integrity of their subject in these debates. Politicians, historians and public commentators have also been leading campaigners for Australian history teaching over the last twenty years at least. But if we all agree Australian history's important, why is it so difficult to reach a consensus on the topic? Why do these history wars keep breaking out?

Australian history teaching is so contested because, despite the country's different education systems, it's the only place where everyone comes into contact with it. We don't have to remember it and we certainly don't have to like it, but we do have to learn it in one form or another. While our first encounters with Australian history are likely to come from our families, from television or other media, school is the only place where young people are formally presented with their nation's past.[13] The stakes are high when it comes to teaching 'our story' to the next generation of Australians – that's why everyone seems to have something to say.

Well, almost everyone. Politicians, historians and various pundits all have an opinion on what kids should learn and how they should learn it, but where are the kids themselves in all of this? Eighteen per cent don't know who Edmund Barton was; 23 per cent don't know the meaning of Australia Day. We all know what students don't know about the nation's history. But we're less clear on what they *do* know. For instance, how do they engage with Australia's past?[14]

History's children

The easiest way to find out what kids think about Australian history is to ask them, and that's essentially what this book does: it's a series of interviews with groups of students, as well as teachers and curriculum officials, about teaching Australian history. *History's Children* is the culmination of a research project that went into the classroom to find out how kids connect with the past. We know what's in the syllabus documents and we know the scope of public debate (because it keeps breaking out all around us). But it's less clear how students and teachers relate to Australian history. As we've already seen, just because Australian history is interesting to *us*, students aren't necessarily engaging with it in class.

The idea for this research initially came from Tony Taylor, a history educationist at Monash University, who co-ordinated the original grant application to the Australian Research Council (ARC) in 2004. I came in having just finished a PhD on debates about teaching Australian history at school and was fortunate enough to get a postdoctoral fellowship from the ARC to conduct this research. There were four of us altogether – as well as Tony and myself, Carmel Young from the University of Sydney and Stuart Macintyre from the University of Melbourne all helped conceive the project in its early stages. We defined the parameters of the research and the scope of the project in Australia as well as developing a comparative study in Canada, which will also be published. Tony supervised the project and has generously assisted its progress and direction. Carmel and Stuart have also been integral to its development. Each gave total support to this research, reading drafts and discussing its central ideas – it certainly couldn't have been completed without them. But the writing of this book, and any mistakes within it, are my own.

The project was developed in response to some of these very public and political debates over Australian history education. It was never intended to be a statistical analysis of students' historical knowledge; we seem to have enough of them already. Instead, we wanted to explore some of the ways in which students connect with the past. What do they find interesting about Australian history? What don't they enjoy? Do they think it should be a compulsory subject? If so, how should it be taught?

In all, 246 people from around Australia were interviewed: there were 182 high school students (all but two were interviewed in small focus groups), as well as forty-three teachers (including five student teachers) and twenty curriculum officials from around Australia.[15] One former federal curriculum manager was also interviewed. As I mentioned, this isn't a strictly representative sample – it's a broad collection of interviews about teaching the nation's history. We wanted the project to present a range of voices from the classroom, rather than tables of survey results.

So the main requirement was a diversity of students and teachers across the country. It was essential that schools nationwide be visited, and that different classes from different school sectors be represented. Eventually, we decided to visit four schools in each state and territory. I went to work applying for ethics clearance from the university and the different education systems, and also contacted history teachers and curriculum boards. Eleven ethics proposals were completed for this project (eight in Australia and three in Canada), as well as various police checks and permissions to visit the schools and conduct the interviews. While teachers and students were given pseudonyms as part of this ethics process, and their schools are not identified, the names of curriculum officials and education department representatives have been kept because they're in public positions and their interviews focus on official policy.

We canvassed whether to visit primary schools or high schools and eventually decided to speak with students from years 9–12. For a start, that's where most Australian history is explicitly taught in school. Furthermore, secondary teachers of history are much more likely to have been trained in history education, which is critical to get a professional sense of how to teach the subject well.[16] The middle to upper years of high school are also where students are most likely to have a comparable understanding of their nation's past. In the primary years, Australian history usually begins by looking at families and local communities. Towards the beginning of this research I did speak with a terrific group of primary school students and their teacher in Tasmania. Their responses show that children as young as nine or ten have opinions about learning their nation's past that warrant further investigation. But that study will have to wait.

We decided to speak with students in small focus groups, rather than individually, so that the interview process wouldn't be too intimidating for them. Alone, students might feel the interview was more like an interrogation or a test than a chat about Australian history. Conversely, in too large a group their individual voices might become lost. So the average size of the groups was about five or six, and this seemed to provide a fairly good balance between gauging students' individual opinions and generating discussion between them.

Certainly there were quieter students and more engaged ones. I really struggled to get some groups talking – and I remember one particular group of students in Hobart looking at me suspiciously, perhaps thinking 'why does *she* care about history?' Yet there were other groups I couldn't stop, and I had to rein them in before the class time was up. Teachers sat in on only two of the student interviews, as most thought their presence might unduly influence what their students said. But even in those two interviews, I noticed that the students spoke freely and didn't seem fazed by their teacher's presence. Most interviews with these student focus groups went for about thirty minutes – they usually took place during one of their history classes or at lunchtime so that their daily timetable wasn't unduly interrupted. Interviews with teachers also depended on their classes for the day and tended to go for thirty minutes to an hour.

While this isn't necessarily a representative sample, I can vouch that it's a broad one. I spent all of 2006 travelling around Australia, visiting places I'd never seen and parachuting myself into various history classes. Many were similar to my own school experiences growing up in inner Sydney. Of course, there were differences too: some schools had more resources than I could ever imagine; others, meanwhile, were dealing with cultural and social issues that seemed impossible to comprehend.

In the end I visited thirty-four high schools (four each from Queensland, South Australia, Western Australia, the Australian Capital Territory, Tasmania and Victoria; and five each from New South Wales and the Northern Territory). Twenty-two of these were public schools (including a single-sex public school in Sydney and a selective school); there were also twelve non-government schools (both single-sex and co-educational), which included nine Christian or Catholic schools, one Islamic and two non-denominational institutions. Most schools were in or near major cities, but I also visited five schools from rural or remote areas in New South Wales, the Northern Territory, Tasmania and Victoria.

Among the participants, females are slightly over-represented, and this is particularly noticeable among the teachers I spoke with, 65 per cent of whom were female. In Australian high schools in 2006, women made up almost 57 per cent of the teaching force (although it's likely that figure is slightly higher in the humanities). Non-government schools made up 37 per cent of secondary schools that I visited, compared with 42 per cent of secondary schools nationally in 2006.[17]

Furthermore, I didn't visit a full range of schools in each state and territory – so South Australia and Western Australia were over-represented by more successful independent and public schools, for example, while Tasmania and the Northern Territory had a larger leaning towards public schools that weren't so academically oriented. While the balance is about right in total, taken regionally, the schools I visited may seem skewed towards particular school sectors or socio-economic groups. And I certainly couldn't reach every type of school in Australia – what about Steiner schools, or kids in remote Indigenous communities, or even home-schooled students? I would love to have kept going, but there comes a point when your funding and energy run out and it's time to come home and start writing.

While I tried to arrange interviews with state, territory and federal education ministers, I didn't get to speak with any of them, unfortunately. Some ministers' offices directed me to their curriculum bodies or bureaucratic departments. Others were probably too busy to speak at all and left it at that. It's understandable, I guess, when politicians' diaries no doubt fill up months in advance. But given the intense public interest in the subject, and politicians' frequent commentary on it, it would have been interesting to hear how they actively negotiate their governments' policies about Australian history teaching with the competing demands of their constituents, the media, education unions and curriculum bodies.

When it came to dealing with schools I had much more luck. I began by contacting the various history teachers' associations around the country, which gave me lists of different schools I might try, and I went off to contact the relevant teachers and principals. The response from schools was overwhelmingly positive. They were genuinely interested in the research and kindly accommodated my visits and interviews.

Using these professional associations as my contact base meant that the teachers I spoke with were actively engaged with the subject – they're the teachers who go off to history teaching conferences and keep up to date with professional development, whether they've been teaching history as a stand-alone subject or via SOSE. Collectively, they expressed a real passion for the subject, and their love of history and their experience teaching it comes through strongly in the book.

On the other hand, contacting teachers through their subject associations meant that I didn't speak with any teachers who really hate the subject or teachers who have no history background and have been lumped with an Australian history class due to timetable constraints. We know such situations exist because teachers have spoken about them – to me and others. When Tony Taylor was researching his National Inquiry into School History, he heard of one history class in which the teacher came in, dumped his books and said, 'I'm a geography teacher, I hate history'.[18]

One of the teachers I spoke with said that a physical education teacher at her school taught medieval history. And a former history teacher said that she remembered a teacher at her school who 'sat in the staff room and said: "I don't know why I've got all of this [history teaching], I don't have any history background".'[19] These are the staff who slip under the radar: they don't join professional associations because they don't consider themselves history teachers, and they don't stay in the subject long enough to become experienced. Ultimately, it's the classroom that suffers.

The teachers I interviewed may have been committed to the subject, but their kids were much more varied in their historical engagement. Although I requested a spread of students in my initial contact with teachers, there was a possibility that they would ask only their best students to speak with me and the conversation would inevitably focus on how much they loved the subject (and their teacher). But that didn't happen at all. For every student who enjoyed Australian history, there were many more who really disliked it. The subject can't seem to shake its poor reputation among students, and even those who chose history in their senior years were often highly critical of Australian history in particular. Zoran, a year 11 student from Canberra, said he hated Australian history so much that now he studies history 'that deliberately isn't Australia-based'.[20]

Zoran was by no means the exception. In fact, it's fair to say that kids and their teachers over all were remarkably candid in their interviews about what they thought of the subject. I have over 200 000 words of transcripts from these interviews. And time and again, students talked about being 'bored' by their nation's history: it hasn't been taught with any consistency, there's significant topic repetition, and they frequently complained about a lack of exciting material. Teachers, too, are wary of pressing too much Australian history into these reluctant youngsters. So are kids simply sick of the subject?

Putting the project into perspective

Surveys confirm young people's poor levels of understanding about Australian history. They even suggest that kids' apparent refusal to connect with that history may impede their connection with the nation itself. How can students vote if they don't understand Australia's political institutions? Can they ever understand contemporary Australian society if they don't learn its past? Such research shows a large cohort struggling with basic historical and political knowledge, but doesn't tell us why.

In fact, when I spoke with the students themselves, it quickly became clear that their disinterest in Australian history wasn't a petulant rejection of their nation, but more a frustration with the way it's been taught. Pia in Sydney complained that learning about Australia's federation had been 'so repetitive' throughout her school years. For Trace, a year 11 student in Brisbane, Indigenous history was much the same. 'Yeah, we just learnt the same thing every year,' she said. 'It wasn't very interesting.'[21] These aren't students who think Australian history's stupid or that school sucks, so why bother learning anything? Australian history is stigmatised because of how they have learnt it, not because they think it's irrelevant.

The interview schedules ranged across students' and teachers' experiences with five Australian history topics: local history, Indigenous history, federation, Australians at war, and contemporary political history. I asked them to discuss each topic in turn – had they ever learnt/taught about it? What did they find interesting/not so interesting? Did they think it was important to know? We chose these key topics because they reflect important themes and timeframes in Australian history and, irrespective of where they attended school, each student was likely to have studied them at some point. This meant we were better able to compare their responses with each other and their teachers.

Those responses were pretty categorical. It didn't matter what school they went to or what region they grew up in, the kids I spoke with said Australian history was often dull and repetitive. The only times students consistently enjoyed the subject was in relation to Australians at war – and it's no coincidence that the topic contains some rich (and gory) material and deals with monumental events when Australians were taking part in world-changing affairs. Apart from those global historic moments, however, students seemed turned off by a lot of Australian history. Jake, a year 11 student from

Brisbane, was blunt in his judgement: 'If they pretended there was a civil war, it would be much more interesting,' he said. 'But there wasn't, so it's boring.'²²

A comment like that almost makes you feel like giving up. After all, what's the point of teaching Australian history if it can never match the thrills of the French Revolution or the American Civil War? But along with dismissive remarks like Jake's came a whole swag of student responses about the need to teach Australian history in schools. After discussing the five history topics, students were then asked questions about their attitudes to Australian history, and history more broadly: Do they enjoy Australian history? Do they think it should be a compulsory subject? How do they learn history best? And would they change anything about the way history is taught at their school?

In this second section of the interviews students were frequently confounded by their earlier (often negative) comments about Australian history, because here they all tended to agree that it *should* be taught. Just because many kids haven't enjoyed learning the subject doesn't mean they don't sense its significance. When I asked a group of year 12 students in Darwin whether Australian history ought to be compulsory, all of them said yes – in unison – although you can also see their collective agreement came with some qualifications:

> ***Do you think Australian history should be a compulsory school subject?***
>
> **All:** *Yes.*
>
> **Daniel:** *Australia and otherwise, yes.*
>
> **Gabby:** *Maybe not necessarily at a year 12 level, but in the compulsory years of high school.*

> *Tani: But they've got to spruce it up because I remember learning heaps of Australian history earlier on and I just was so bored by it.*[23]

Students may not respond with resounding energy to Australia's past, but they certainly understand its value in schools. Yasmin, a year 10 student from an Islamic school in western Sydney, said history 'can make you understand what is happening now and what influenced it to happen in the past.' 'Yeah,' said her classmate Ramah, 'history's all around us. Like you wouldn't see someone going on the news and talking about *maths*.'[24]

For their part, teachers were also caught between this widely acknowledged need for the subject and getting their kids interested. Cameron teaches at a Catholic boys' school in Perth and was committed to engaging his students in any way he could. 'I think that the key to making history enjoyable is to make it interesting,' he said, 'and you've got to make it interesting by not focusing on facts and figures and those sorts of things. You've got to make it real.' For Stephanie in Tasmania, generating students' interest was also the critical way to get them involved: 'if I was to sit down and say, okay, now in seventeen dum de dum this is what happened, and dum de dum de dum de dum ... I mean that would be boring.'[25]

Each of these interviews provides a snapshot into a classroom, a school and often a whole community. I've spent the last five years studying Australian history education at university, so it's been refreshing to have this 'coalface' experience with history classes around the country that have to deal with these questions about teaching and learning Australian history every day. And to be honest, I hadn't anticipated what it would be like to return to school – it certainly brought back a lot of memories about my own history education.

I'm also very aware that my voice is quite prominent in the write-up of this research. I didn't set out to produce a sort of travelogue as it were, and no doubt a different researcher would have produced a very different book. But I can't escape the fact that I was visiting these schools and the interviews should be read as students' and teachers' responses to those visits. While many students seemed quite interested to share their thoughts on Australian history education, it's unlikely that they spontaneously talk about the intricacies of the subject to each other without being prompted. As one history teacher from New South Wales joked in his interview, 'They're not going to run round at lunchtime saying, "Guess what I learnt about federation in class?".'[26] In other words, it was inevitable that my presence, irrespective of how detached or discrete I tried to be, would influence how the interviews went.

Sometimes what went on outside the interview was just as interesting. At one boys' school I remember waiting in a classroom while a group of young students jumped up and down outside trying to get a glimpse of their visitor through the rather high glass. 'Is she hot?' one of the shorter ones asked. (I didn't hear the answer.) At a town in central Australia, meanwhile, Aboriginal kids played 'chicken' with the road trains all night outside the window where I was staying. What else did they have to do? Such stories show that each class also has a context that cannot be divorced from the interviews themselves.

After the research and transcribing were complete, working out how to study this material became all-consuming. Some researchers codify their data in a computer program that allows similar ideas to be easily retrieved and compared for further analysis. I did most of the transcribing myself, and did use a database to organise the interviews. But rather than codify it, I embedded myself in the words of the interviews as they stood: I read and re-read files full of transcripts and gradually got a strong sense of the material that lay within them.

I've always been struck by how oral histories and grounded research can paint such a vivid picture of people's experiences and ideas. They have a capacity to illuminate in such different ways from more removed academic research. People's ideas described in their own words are rich and nuanced, and the fieldwork itself takes you to places and allows you to meet people who are living the very story you're trying to tell. That doesn't mean you can simply absorb their narrative or take on their experience as your own. While identifying with a lot of these teachers and students, I was also surprised by many things they said. Consequently, there's a real tension throughout the book between letting the participants 'speak for themselves' and my analysis of them.

I liked the way Judith Brett and Anthony Moran discussed the approach they used in their fascinating study of Australians' political beliefs in *Ordinary People's Politics*: 'Rather than scooping up opinions in huge vats to run through statistical strainers, our engagement is with the voices of individual men and women as they talk about their lives and the place politics has and does not have in them'.[27] Like Brett and Moran, my interest is in the 'voices' themselves – this time from the classroom – as students and teachers talk about the ways they connect with their nation's past.

I don't pretend this study is comprehensive, but it does give us an insight into the history classroom that has been depressingly absent from public debates over the past. When Keith Barton and Linda Levstik described research they conducted into the historical understanding of primary and middle school students in the United States, they were surprised by how interested the kids seemed to be in their project – because they'd been given an opportunity to discuss their opinions about history.[28] I often felt the same interest from students during these interviews; many of them seemed genuinely surprised to be asked their thoughts on Australian history.

It's a shame, then, that they have such little sway in those politicised debates over the subject. This project is by no means the first to head into the classroom, but I do hope that it brings some of these classroom perspectives into the public frame of Australian history education. We probably all have ideas on what kids should know, but do we really have a sense of what *they* think? Whatever our thoughts on history teaching – what to teach and how to teach it – it's in the classroom that it's eventually going to be realised. Students clearly have something to say about learning Australian history, so why aren't they in the debate?

CHAPTER 1

The 'Edmund Barton syndrome'

> *Have you ever been taught about federation?*
>
> **All:** *Yes [groans].*
>
> **Linda:** *I think that needs to be taken out! It was horrible. It's so confusing.*
>
> **Jake:** *It's not exciting.*
>
> **Zach:** *They didn't really go into depth either. It was just like, 'They all got together and decided, this will be Australia,' and that's it.*
>
> Year 11 students, public high school, Brisbane

What sort of nation would forget the name of its first prime minister?

There's a significant public expectation in Australia that children should know the critical facts about their country's foundation, and it's our responsibility to see them taught. Of course, this isn't a uniquely Australian obsession by any means – the 'birth of the nation' is a powerful idea that inspires patriotic interest all over the world. But what happens when your nation's official founding moment is more likely to generate glazed eyes than great passion?

Student after student around the country groaned when I asked them about Australia's federation in their interviews. At a Catholic boys' school in Brisbane, Jeff confessed that for him 'it wasn't an exciting time'. 'Like, I'm a seventeen year old', he explained. 'I don't find governments being formed in 1900 exciting.' Keira goes to a public high school near Darwin and was similarly unimpressed: 'Okay, see, I don't like history and I suck at all that politics and commonwealth and federation whatever.'[1]

Part of the problem seems to be an overwhelming sense among students that federation just doesn't cut it compared with other countries' proud beginnings. Parkes' Tenterfield oration wasn't exactly characterised by bloody violence. And although the federation meetings had their share of argument, animus and distrust, they were hardly revolutionary. It's for these reasons that Alex, who studies year 12 at an Adelaide public school, didn't feel federation was particularly enthralling: 'It was kind of interesting, but really, I find that Australian history doesn't match up to foreign history.' Another year 12 student at a public senior secondary college in Canberra found the topic boring because it's so familiar: 'Because it's just here, it's all around, it isn't that interesting. Like I'm fascinated with

European history, but with Australia it's like, *bleurgh*, because it's always going to be here.'[2]

Even teachers admit they struggle to make federation engaging for their students. Mary, who teaches at a public school in Brisbane, says 'it's boring as bat shit!'. 'Sorry,' she quickly apologises, 'I can't get excited about it, and if I can't get excited about it, how can I make it dramatic and interesting for adolescents?' Ellen from Darwin reckoned students simply don't like the topic 'Because it's boring and political,' she said. 'And kids are not interested in politics ... kids hate it, they really get bored by it, they really do. It's just sort of mind-blowingly dull.'[3]

In fairness to the kids I interviewed, Australians generally aren't renowned for their great or reverential attachment to political history. But that doesn't mean they don't want children to at least learn about it. Repeated surveys about what young people know (or *don't* know) about Australia's past generate predictable outrage and anxiety among politicians and public commentators around the country. And in the lead-up to the centenary of federation in 2001, it was students' knowledge of Australia's political establishment that caused particular angst.

In 1994 a report by the Civics Expert Group (which included the historian Stuart Macintyre and education professionals Ken Boston and Susan Pascoe) published a survey conducted by the polling company, ANOP, run by Rod Cameron. The results showed very poor comprehension of Australia's constitution, for example, as well as its federation and political history. Another report by the University of Sydney educationist Murray Print produced similar findings, and he concluded that 'Students in our schools simply don't possess acceptable levels of political knowledge and understanding to become effective citizens.'[4]

That was just the beginning. In 1997, a survey by the National Council for the Centenary of Federation showed that only 18 per cent of those interviewed knew the name of Australia's first prime minister (Edmund Barton) and 43 per cent of interviewees didn't even know what federation meant.[5] More students knew the presidents of the United States than Australia's own leaders – a worrying enough fact to prompt a national ad campaign that asked: *What sort of nation would forget the name of its first prime minister?*

This preoccupation with students' lack of national knowledge is hardly isolated. Every year it seems there's yet another survey highlighting their historical deficiencies.[6] But the lead-up to 2001 heralded a massive national anniversary: commemorative coins would be issued to all schoolchildren, national days of celebration and re-enactment had been planned, and a wealth of resource materials had been developed for teachers and classrooms. There was little excuse for ignorance about *any* prime minister, let alone Australia's first.

It wasn't just politicians' national pride that was rankled by the survey results. Members of the public also voiced their concerns. In a letter to the Adelaide *Advertiser* in 1999, Julie Beare wrote about a worrying dearth of historical knowledge that had been uncovered by the National Council for the Centenary of Federation. 'What sort of citizens are we producing who have not learnt about our nation's history?' she asked. 'The study of Australian history should be one of the great unifying forces in our nation's life, instead of a forgotten relic in our schools.' Ross Fitzgerald, a Professor of History and Politics at Griffith University, wrote to the Brisbane *Courier Mail* a year later and said there was a great 'need for the proper teaching of history, geography and civics. My experience is that many Australians aged under 30 have been starved of appropriate history teaching.'[7]

The anxiety aroused by the poor survey results should be as unsurprising as the results themselves: kids find federation boring, just as grown-ups insist it be taught and understood.

Such is the troubled relationship over federation that it has been labelled the 'Edmund Barton syndrome' by the history educationist Tony Taylor.[8] It's a paradox that sees many students and teachers avoiding the topic where possible while politicians, historians and the general public insist on its central importance in any school curriculum.

While there's no disputing federation's significance in Australian history, its attractiveness in the classroom isn't quite so assured – despite the passion and debate it generated in the late nineteenth century, federation simply doesn't boast the drama of colonisation, for example, or the violence of the Gallipoli landing or the Western Front. In fact, federation's main selling point is the general consensus that it's *important*. But that alone doesn't seem to be enough for teachers to inspire classroom interest and engagement.

John, the head of history at a public girls' school in Sydney, really struggles to teach the topic well: 'It's not like the United States' constitution, you know, that sort of "liberty and the pursuit of happiness",' he said. 'I find kids are interested in history if they can link up with personalities. But these people, with their big moustaches and high-flown words, and their, you know, extended education and vocabulary, and so forth, it's very hard to get kids to empathise with them in that sense.' Like John, Sarah also finds federation difficult to teach. While she thinks that learning about 'the outcome of federation is important' for students at her independent girls' school in Melbourne, actually engaging them with the topic is another matter: 'I do feel that the criticism it's a lot of Victorian men in beards nattering to each other is fairly justified.'[9]

So the 'Edmund Barton syndrome' has left us in a bit of a bind: the more teachers and students resist doing federation in class, the more anxious politicians, public commentators and parents become about young Australians' connections to their national history. While the survey reports leading up to the 2001 centenary expressed significant concern that students could emerge from their schooling without the historical background or civic knowledge to even vote, deeper questions of national identity and belonging became the underlying focus of public debate: if teachers struggle with the topic as much as their students, how will anyone ever learn Australia's foundation story? And if they don't learn it, will they simply *stop caring*?

My interviews around the country show this is far from the case – both students and teachers sense the great significance of federation in Australia's past. But recognising federation's importance isn't the same as engaging with it. Public anxiety over the state of students' knowledge around the centenary of federation confirmed a widespread belief in the importance of historical comprehension as a national duty almost, where teaching children about the 'critical facts' of Australia's history won't simply create more capable citizens, but prouder ones.

Paradoxically, this is a very *uncritical* view of history teaching because it stresses the important stories, facts and events in Australia's history as innate rather than contingent. And for that reason, you won't find such a view widely represented in professional discussions about the subject. Nevertheless, it figures prominently in popular understandings of the role of history education. At its heart is a belief that history forms an essential element of core national knowledge and identity. And without it, young Australians are endangering their country with their own ignorance.

Such was the level of public concern over the state of national knowledge in the 1990s that successive governments became actively involved in promoting the importance of federation in schools. After the Civics Expert Group had reported their findings in 1994, Paul Keating's Labor Government committed

$25 million over four years to implement its findings. While John Howard's election in 1996 radically changed Australia's political direction, his new Coalition Government continued the civics education momentum initiated by its predecessor. The program was renamed Discovering Democracy in 1997 and was chaired by the historian John Hirst. That same year the federal Education Minister David Kemp announced plans for civics and citizenship to be taught to all school students in years 4–10 as part of a public push to increase knowledge of the nation's history and political processes. 'Young Australians must gain a sound knowledge of the evolution of our pioneering democracy if its success and vigour is to survive in the next century,' he insisted. He also commissioned a National Inquiry into history teaching because he was concerned 'that, as we approach the centenary of federation, the study of history was declining in our schools,' and he subsequently committed $2.3 million for a Commonwealth History Project – one of the inquiry's recommendations.[10]

It's difficult to fully clarify the various motives for boosting Australian history around 2001: the timing (leading up to the centenary) was obviously a catalyst, as was the publication of the survey results that revealed such poor levels of historical comprehension. But it's much harder to tease out the relationship between the public and the political anxieties over the past, which the research reports both prompted and reinforced. Concern over the state of national knowledge is deeply felt by many Australians – citizens *and* politicians. But to what extent did the public anxiety shape the political response? And to what extent did the political response (both Labor's and the Coalition's) capitalise on public anxiety?

A wealth of education-related literature and materials was produced following the massive government effort to fund and promote the teaching of Australia's federation. The National Council for the Centenary of Federation publicised the centenary and supported the implementation of federation-related activities in schools. A civics and citizenship website was produced by the federal Department of Employment, Education, Training and Youth Affairs (now the Department of Education, Science and Training). And various resources, such as *One Destiny! The Federation Story Centenary Edition* and the *Discovering Democracy* kits were sent out to all schools. Meanwhile, Australian Readers, filled with juicy historical sources and information, were produced for teachers and students around the country.

All this was surely a worthy attempt to battle the 'Edmund Barton syndrome', but what impact did it actually have in classrooms? Did the public and political anxiety over students' knowledge of federation effect any real change in student interest and engagement? After interviewing teachers and students, I'm not so sure. Beyond recognising the name of our first prime minister, for example, I'm not convinced that students have begun to engage critically with Australia's federation history.

Connecting to Federation

While it's clear many teachers benefited from the extra resources that were being pumped into schools, it's harder to say whether the materials alleviated students' resistance to learning federation, or the public anxiety over young Australians' historical knowledge for that matter. Marco, who teaches at a public high school in outer Melbourne, found himself surprised by the usefulness of the materials that accompanied the course. 'I always thought, "Oh that's pretty tedious",' he related in his interview. 'But there is a lot of good stuff out there and there was a good kit – the Federation Resource Kit – and yeah, I did a little unit and I thought it'd be pretty dreary, but it wasn't too bad.'[11]

Marco's experience was by no means universal, however, and a few teachers I spoke with said that although the federation resources were certainly visible, they didn't seem to change their students' attitudes to the topic. Sally takes a year 12 Australian history class at a small rural school in central Victoria, but has never had any luck with federation. Even in 2001, her students didn't enjoy the topic at all: 'During the Centennial [sic] a lot of kits came out and the government put out lots of school resources, and again ... I don't know whether this is the way it was taught, but the kids just got sick to death of it and hated it.'[12]

Considering the variety and richness of these resources, it's a shame they didn't have the impact in schools that various governments and curriculum bodies no doubt envisaged. Neil, a Canberra history teacher, thought that part of the problem was the use of the materials, rather than the materials themselves: '*Discovering Democracy* is a great resource, but too frequently it's sitting on principals' shelves because good teachers didn't need it and bad teachers didn't know it existed.'[13]

So despite the considerable efforts to develop and implement federation resources, many of the teachers I spoke with expressed a real reluctance to use the topic as the basis for Australian history in their classes. This isn't to say that teachers don't sense the importance of federation – in fact, they frequently insisted on its critical place in Australia's history. But just acknowledging its worth hasn't been enough to enable teachers to generate any lasting interest in federation among their students.

Daniel teaches at a Catholic boys' school in Brisbane and says that federation 'can be dry, and you sort of do it to some degree as a duty'. He went on: 'You sort of think, "Well you've got to teach your own history," but trying to make it interesting for students is not easy, because there's not the sort of action and excitement in the same way there is with other events.' Elizabeth taught history for many years at a Canberra high school and was exasperated as she explained her various teaching approaches to the topic: 'I can truthfully say I have tried every way I can think of to make federation fascinating and it's not easy!'[14]

For students themselves, meanwhile, the centenary of federation promotions had the desired effect at one level: if kids didn't know about Australia's first prime minister before 2001, they certainly do now. When I asked a group of students at a public school in Hobart if they could remember anything they'd learnt about federation, Emma piped up, laughing: 'Edmund Barton! ... It was on TV!' She wasn't the only one. Morgan, a year 10 student at an independent girls' school in Canberra, scoffed that someone might have actually missed him in class: 'It's like, to be politically correct today you've got to have a basic outline, and everyone knows who Edmund Barton is!'[15]

While students at a small school in south-eastern Tasmania struggled to identify the details about federation, they definitely remembered the medal they received as part of the centenary celebrations:

> *Have any of you learnt about Australia's federation?*
>
> **Hayley:** *I don't really remember much about it. I remember getting a federation medallion.*
>
> **Steve:** [aside] *What's federation?*
>
> **Stefan:** [aside] *It's when all the states came together to become Australia.*
>
> *Did you enjoy learning about it?*
>
> **Karen:** *The fact that we can't remember any of it sort of shows that we weren't really paying any attention.*[16]

From the interview, it's pretty easy to see that these students know they're *supposed* to understand federation. They even acknowledged the importance of learning about it ('because it's part of Australia's history,' says Matt later in the interview), but they showed very little connection to the topic itself.

This is where interpreting their interview gets complicated. On the one hand, it's quite possible to read their comments from a perspective that sees their lack of interest in federation as foolish and ignorant. You could say such a position reflects the significant popular belief in the importance of core national knowledge among Australia's youth. On the other hand, to be fair to these kids, they were far from ignorant. They were great to talk with – they were funny, honest and engaging. In fact, they were one of the most memorable groups I spoke with because they were so lively and, with one exception, they all clearly *enjoyed* history, including topics like Australians at war, Indigenous history and the history of their community. They simply found federation boring.

When I interviewed their teacher afterwards she said that unless she could connect her kids to federation history, they simply wouldn't engage with it:

> I don't think federation is ... a topic that would really grab them. Possibly if they did they'd do it from the local perspective, like what did the saw millers, the loggers and the fishermen and the berry pickers and the farmers think about federation, and what did it mean to them in 1901 without iPods and faxes and you know? ... the creation of the nation as we know it in the constitution, I mean obviously it's extremely important to all Australians and it is an interesting story, but how do you connect a kid with that?[17]

In other words, kids don't want history they can't connect with. This doesn't mean that the facts shouldn't be taught,

Gail acknowledged, or that issues of national knowledge aren't important. But if students are going to *learn* Australian history, it has to 'really grab them', as she suggests. While it may well be 'politically correct' to know about Edmund Barton and federation, unless students can find ways into the topic they can relate to, it's going to remain abstract and removed.

This problem of connecting kids to federation is even more pressing in remote areas, where attendance and even basic literacy are critical, everyday educational concerns. Justine teaches at a large public school in central Australia, but hasn't even tried to get her mostly Indigenous students to understand the intricacies of federation: 'If you go straight into a whole list of prime ministers and things like that, it doesn't have any relevance to them,' she said, 'so I think here, particularly, you've got to cater for what the kids can kind of relate to somehow.' When I asked her what she thought federation meant for them, she said 'that kind of thing here is less important than maybe it would be in Canberra'. It is 'much more important for the Indigenous students to learn about the gaining of their rights,' she believed, and 'much more important for them to learn about when the children were taken away and what's happened there'.[18]

Again, we can take these comments in a couple of ways. In one sense, they surely reinforce any public anxiety about the state of historical knowledge among young people. The fact that Justine hasn't taught federation is a worrying reminder of what kids don't know about their own country. But she's also right, of course: what's the point of memorising Edmund Barton as Australia's first prime minister when the most basic educational needs of her students still need to be met?

The challenge of teaching federation isn't confined to disadvantaged or remote schools. During the interviews it became pretty clear that there's a real stigma about Australian history among young people, and federation in particular. You only have to look back on some of those quotes from students early in this chapter to see how they criticise federation's dullness compared with the revolutions and wars that other countries had the (rather perverse) fortune to experience. As a year 11 student from Adelaide tersely remarked, 'There's nothing exciting like guns or arguments or yelling [in federation]. It's just people sat down at a table and decided it.'[19]

When I asked students at a senior secondary college in Canberra whether they had ever studied Australia's federation, Damien replied, 'Yeah, we've done heaps on that.' Patrick jumped straight in: 'It's *so bad*,' he said. A group of year 12 students in Perth were similarly dismissive. Garry explained that he had 'looked at it extensively in primary school during the centenary of federation'. 'In 2001, yeah,' added his classmate Maddison. 'But I never fully understood what it was. I just thought, "*Ugh*, federation" – it wasn't explained to me.'[20]

All this means it's the teachers who are caught between public and political expectations of what students *should* know, and the reality of the classroom where student interest and engagement are not so easily prescribed. While we all may want students to know the critical facts of Australia's history, the challenge is to then teach this knowledge in an engaging and meaningful way.

Yet the difficulty of connecting students with federation has been compounded by problems with the curriculum itself, which has led to significant topic repetition, particularly between primary and secondary schools. It's clear from these interviews that a lot of Australian history really hasn't been taught well, or with any great consistency. And it isn't just students who are saying so. In the last decade alone, research into Australian history education has revealed countless horror stories about its delivery in schools. Australian history teaching is largely unsystematic – there is endless repetition, unstimulating material and a lack of curriculum co-ordination.[21] And federation is no exception.

This has certainly been the experience for Sal, a year 12 student at a public high school in Perth. *Did you enjoy learning about federation?* I asked. 'Maybe the first time, but not for the twenty-seventh time,' she said with exaggerated emphasis. 'I think it was beyond the point of whether or not you enjoyed it, it's just knowing it now, because you learn it *every year*, and you just know it. It's not whether you enjoy it any more.' Even in New South Wales, where one hundred hours of Australian history are prescribed in years 9 and 10, students still complained of topic repetition. Kate, a year 11 student at a public girls' school in Sydney, said that she 'saw the same film about the states' different railway lines about six times!' It's not that it's 'boring,' said her classmate Pia, 'but I think it's because it's so repetitive'.[22]

At a public school in Darwin, the mood among some year 12 students was even more critical:

> *Have you ever been taught about Australia's federation?*
>
> **Tani:** *I can't ever remember learning about federation before this year.*
>
> **Natalie:** *I remember doing it heaps in primary school and it was really boring, and it still is, and Australian history just makes me want to cry. It's so boring and I can't stand it.*
>
> **Tani:** *I have to agree. I do find it more boring than all the European history.*
>
> **Daniel:** *Well, there isn't more than two hundred years' worth.*
>
> **Gabby:** *And because there isn't a lot, you have to focus on things like federation.*[23]

I have only copied out a fraction of the reams of 'federation is soooo boring' quotes that litter my desk – a prevailing mood about a history topic if ever there was. However, it would be a real mistake to only read from these interviews that students can't be bothered learning about federation, or that they think it shouldn't be taught altogether. Sometimes students struggled to find the right words to talk about the importance of learning history, and when they did, it was often slightly glib or clichéd. They frequently explained history's importance in terms of 'learning from our past mistakes', for example, or 'getting to know how we came to where we are today'. But students overwhelmingly identified federation as an important part of Australia's history – and that meant acknowledging it should be taught.

These students from a Catholic boys' school in Adelaide were adamant about the need to teach federation in school:

> *Is it important to learn about federation?*
>
> **Kane:** *Yes, it probably is important because it shows how we federated and became our own sort of independent country.*
>
> **Olaf:** *It's important because it's part of our history. It's a very big part in fact, how Australia became a country, and I think it would be important for most people to know about.*[24]

Even Kate from Sydney, who had complained of repeated topics on federation, said that it was important to know about because 'it's hard for us to imagine how all the different nations, sorry states, were separate, because we've grown up in a country where we're all like *one* country'. 'You kind of have to understand and appreciate that we came together as a whole country,' she said, 'but I didn't find it that interesting.'[25] A group of year 10 students from an independent girls' school in Canberra felt just as strongly about federation's significance:

> **Do you think it's important to know about federation?**
>
> **All:** *Yeah.*
>
> **Morgan:** *It's the basis of like, our country.*
>
> **Annie:** *Our nation.*
>
> **Morgan:** *Of the way it is now.*[26]

In so many of these interviews students aren't afraid to voice their (often critical) views on the topic of federation, but they're equally certain of its significance. *Do you think it is important to learn about federation?* I asked a group of year 12 boys at a Brisbane Catholic school. 'Yeah,' replied Arthur. 'I think it's important. If you live in Australia you should know about it.' At an Islamic school in western Sydney, Nada was similarly attuned in her response: 'Well, it's important to know how we actually got here in politics.'[27] And if students are willing to acknowledge the importance of learning federation in school, the challenge is to actually engage them.

But what about Australia's second prime minister?

A few months after John Howard's Australia Day speech in 2006 calling for a 'root and branch renewal' of Australian history teaching, the federal Education Minister Julie Bishop also urged a 'renaissance' in the subject. 'Not enough students are learning Australian history,' she said, 'and there is too much political bias and not enough pivotal facts and dates being taught.' Bishop outlined the sort of history she felt Australian children should be learning:

> *Every schoolchild should know, for example, when and why the then Lieutenant James Cook sailed along the east coast of Australia. Every child should know why the British transported convicts to Australia and who Australia's first prime minister was. They should also know how and why federation came about, and why we were involved in the two world wars.*[28]

After her comments, I started asking students and teachers about this idea of 'knowledge' – is federation just something you have to *know*, or can it be made interesting? Is it like learning your times tables – boring at the time, but you'll be grateful later? The responses from teachers were quite varied on this, as they reflected on their own experiences and on their students.

Some teachers think there is only so much you can do with a topic like federation. At a senior secondary college in Canberra, Neil sensed the limitations of teaching it in class:

> *So how do we overcome this tension between the expectation that students should know about federation, and that fact that many students find it boring? Do we just have to knuckle down and do it?*
>
> *To a degree yes. Peter Stanley [the Principal Historian at the Australian War Memorial] has made reference to the idea of 'recognition knowledge'. That is, sufficient knowledge to know that it happened, and if they want to take it further they can dig down into the details themselves. I think federation is one of those things where if you achieve recognition knowledge, you've probably gone as far as you can.*[29]

In other words, federation is ultimately limited by the interest it can generate, Neil suggests, compared with other topics such as Australians at war or Nazi Germany. He thinks it's much easier to spark up a class debate over a topic like the Anzac Legend because kids are naturally interested in the drama of conflict. Other teachers have had similar experiences. Federation 'is one of those topics that they sit through just because we say "You have to do it",' agrees Tamsyn, a teacher at a public high school in Canberra. 'I have found that they don't engage with it at all.'[30]

But there were also teachers and curriculum designers who wondered whether the factual emphasis on federation was actually undermining the topic. Elouise teaches history at an independent girls' school in Perth and stressed the importance of teaching a coherent national narrative. 'Way too many kids are leaving school without being able to converse [about] the nation because they know nothing about it,' she said. But Elouise was also anxious to see that any emphasis on knowledge was not that alone, and she wondered whether the push to teach the topic during the centenary in 2001 might have over-emphasised a rather narrow understanding of the subject. 'Yeah, I think they need to be aware of it,' she agreed, but 'I'd love them to know who the second prime minister was.'[31]

So there seems to be a real tension here between public expectations to teach kids Australian history because it's 'good for them' and teaching them something they can critically engage with. Like Elouise, Tony Brian-Davis, a history teacher who previously managed the federal government's Commonwealth History Project, also emphasised the importance of a more sophisticated historical engagement. He accepts that 'people should know who Edmund Barton was,' he says, 'but in fact we need to know what Edmund Barton and federation was about and, you know, what was there before federation?' To that end, students need to be asked 'What was the referendum about? And how did Edmund Barton end up being prime minister?'³²

Some students even suggest that an over-emphasis on 'the facts' has exacerbated the stigma about federation. While many of them dutifully remembered the first prime minister in their interviews around the country, a few wondered if there shouldn't be a little bit more to the subject than that. At a public school in suburban Brisbane, Miranda griped that history shouldn't just be about knowing one or two facts. She knew that federation was in 1901, and that Barton was Australia's first prime minister, but commented: 'We never did anything after that ... Like I know the name of the first prime minister, but that's the only prime minister I really know, Edmund Barton, and I don't know anything about him, I just know his name. And I don't know anything about any of the other prime ministers.'³³

So long as federation remains a 'fact' to be learnt it will remain dull and disconnected for students, as this year 12 group from Brisbane suggest:

> Do you think Australian history should be a compulsory school subject?
>
> **Arthur:** *Yes.*
>
> **Adrian:** *It depends how you look at it. If you look at history as a times tables sort of thing, then yes.*
>
> **Arthur:** *I don't think it should be to the extent that American history has been taught. Like I think it should still be taught from the perspective that it's open to interpretation.*
>
> **Brendan:** *Yeah, I think if it's compulsory, it shouldn't be inward-looking like America, and I think it should be the whole investigative sort of history. I don't like*

> the idea of just learning facts, and then being told what to think.
>
> **Jeff:** *Because that would be boring.*[34]

Unfortunately, it seems teaching federation has become a bit of a self-fulfilling problem for Australian history education: students think federation's dull, so teachers don't feel they can engage their class, and so students remain disconnected. This is no easy circle to break. But while many teachers had become resigned to teaching the story of federation without any expectations of classroom engagement, some of their colleagues wondered whether it could be done differently. 'I know it's important, but it's a dry history in some ways,' said Deborah, a history teacher from Canberra, and she wondered 'if perhaps there's a way for it to be taught in a more interesting way.'[35]

Brian, a history teacher from the New South Wales Central Coast, refused to admit defeat with federation. He insists that *anything* can be made interesting when it's connected to the students themselves. By 'taking it from the kids' perspective,' he said, '*that* creates interest in the time, and federation becomes part of that background of the time.' If teachers expect federation to be dull, it will be dull: 'I hate teachers who just stand up and say (and I've seen them do it), "We've got to do federation now. This is really boring, but we've got to do it." And, surprise, the kids find it boring.'[36]

Other teachers talk from a similar perspective about engaging their students. 'We try to put it into a context that's got a connection,' says Stephanie, a Hobart high school teacher. Sandra, who teaches at a public senior school in Perth, feels that students 'want to learn' Australian history, but often their experience has been 'quite ad hoc and if it's taught badly it really impedes their willingness to learn it again. Kids learn that if it's boring, you know, why bother doing it.' Instead, history has to 'actually be *about the students*'.[37]

Such comments point to a way forward, where knowing 'what happened' and 'doing history' aren't mutually exclusive. By connecting students to their history, as Brian assures, anything can be made engaging and relevant. I don't want to understate the difficulties of such an approach. Obviously it requires considerable curriculum co-ordination, the support of schools and teachers, as well as a change in the public debates about learning federation. But it's clear that if nothing's done, federation will simply keep sagging for students. While federation will always struggle to generate the passionate classroom excitement of other, bloodier and more revolutionary history topics, simply ticking it off like a shopping list won't generate any lasting engagement either.

Perhaps unsurprisingly, students themselves expressed similar sentiments in their interviews. Caitlin, a year 10 student from an independent girls' school in Melbourne, found federation 'really boring' because they just got taught facts. 'But what could make it really interesting could be to study *why*,' she proposed. 'I don't actually know enough about why Australia federated, why they felt the need to break away.' Morgan, a year 10 student from an independent girls' school in Canberra, described it in similar terms: 'when you're learning about federation it just feels like you're going through the motions – this happened, this happened, this happened, this caused this, and that happened,' she said. 'We looked at reasons for federation, but we don't really have personal histories of the people that brought that along. It's just a sort of stated *fact*.'[38]

Some kids couldn't resist suggesting something a little more humorous, and they obviously relished the opportunity to say what they thought about the subject without being taken too seriously. These year 12 students from Darwin thought that maybe a musical approach might liven up the topic a bit:

> *Despite your experiences learning about federation, do you think it's important to know?*
>
> **Natalie:** *I think it's really important to know.*
>
> **Adrian:** *Yeah, I do think it's important.*
>
> **Gabby:** *They just have to spruce it up a bit.*
>
> **Adrian:** *I reckon they should have a musical, a massive stage production of federation.*
>
> **Tani:** *A cabaret.*
>
> **Adrian:** *I'd like to see guys with really big beards dancing across stage, [singing] 'We want to be free from England'.*
>
> **Natalie:** *I think a really good way of teaching students is through activities and actually breaking up that kind of droll type thing.*[39]

Some students in Brisbane thought that by concentrating on Edmund Barton, maybe they had missed out on some other interesting characters in Australia's political history. 'I know about the one who disappeared,' said Chloe, referring to Harold Holt. Molly jumped in: 'The one who went swimming!' 'They should teach us about that,' agreed Miranda. *'That's amusing!'*[40]

These students were obviously having a bit of fun here, making federation informal and ridiculous enough for them to get interested in the topic. But their comments shouldn't be dismissed as flippant or childish – for it's precisely that sense of enjoyment that can help us think about how students connect with the past. 'We want to be free from England' sings a bearded federalist in Adrian's imaginary musical; sure, it's a little silly, but it shows that too much content can simply kill the subject.

Some kids didn't joke around to make the same point.

'There's a misconception of history that it's just facts and dates,' says Les, a year 10 student from a public school on the New South Wales Central Coast. And in his experience, 'federation confirms that. It kind of overlooks the fact that history's about the people, not just the events, the culture.' By going beyond the facts, Les suggested, federation would be more interesting and better understood. 'History's more than just dates – that's just one part of history. Like why would you need to learn a date if you don't know how you got there? You're not going to fully understand it.'[41]

There's no doubt that federation is a critical part of Australia's story, essential to any understanding of who we are – that's why the apparent apathy young people have about Australian civics and citizenship arouses so much public and political anxiety. Despite its importance in Australia's history, however, students continue to dismiss the topic and insist that it's boring and overly repetitive. Despite all the effort and all the teaching resources about federation that have been released over the last ten years, student attitudes to the topic remain pretty dismissive.

But why is this? Why do students still find federation boring, and the latest research into students' knowledge continue to show parlous levels of understanding about Australia's political history?[42] It seems the problem is a lack of genuine classroom engagement. Ensuring that students can name Australia's first prime minister may well be a popular political gesture, but without fostering any real connection to that history it's just another 'boring' topic that classes continue to skirt over or avoid altogether. The 'Edmund Barton syndrome' may have got the media going, and more of us remember the name of our first prime minister, but it seems there's still a way to go before students are genuinely interested in federation.

CHAPTER 2

The allure of Anzac

> **Is it important to learn about Australia's war history?**
>
> **Edie:** *World War I sort of forged the Australian identity, so it's important that we know about it.*
>
> **Anthony:** *It's an important part of our history. If it wasn't for World War I we'd probably still be fighting under the British and under the Queen.*
>
> **Beth:** *Yeah, it's about Australia's history, like where Australia comes from.*
>
> Year 10 students, public high school, central Australia

The 'Australian Mecca'

In 2006 *The Age* ran a rather sweet piece about a Melbourne school student who had just won a place on the annual Spirit of Anzac prize – a state government program designed to encourage young Victorians to honour Australia's wartime sacrifices. I read the article one morning and cut it out as an example of the language young people use to describe their national identity. Sarah Noori had arrived in Australia as a refugee from Afghanistan as an eight year old. Now in year 10, she was touring war sites and memorials in Singapore, Vietnam and Japan with a group of other Victorian students. Noori described her own experiences as a refugee being welcomed to Australia in the context of the Anzac story: 'Being here is my way of saying to the world that the spirit of Anzac – determination, generosity and kindness – is still relevant [to] Australians today.'[1]

Many of the students I spoke with ascribed a similar national significance to Australia's war history. While federation is dismissed for its dry, political and overly factual emphasis, students see the Anzac story as rich and vivid. For Ramah, a year 10 student from Sydney, war is interesting because it's an 'international' topic, she said, 'plus you have the issue of death and killings. Like, you can't ignore that! In federation, you wouldn't see people killing themselves to get what they want. Whereas in the wars, people actually go and defend their country, and that's like more dramatic, you know.'[2]

Teachers were also taken with students' interest in war history. John teaches history at a public girls' school in Sydney, and says that his students 'enjoy the war, certainly more than federation':

> They can link with the experiences of people under the stress of threat to life, conscription. They can link to

women protesting about their sons going off to war. These are very personal things that generate strong emotions. The documents are good, there's plenty of graphics, and they're not so far removed that they appear to be starchy old men in top hats – that sort of thing – and they do come away with a memory of that.[3]

With so much action and drama it's easy to see why studying the Anzacs at Gallipoli or the muddy, futile heroism of the Western Front excites classes full of kids more than a constitutional convention. But I wasn't expecting them to express such passion when they talked about the topic. When I asked a group of students at a Catholic boys' school in Perth whether they had ever learnt about Australians at war, Robert said he 'found it to be the best Australian history that … we've done, because it was just more interesting. It was more exciting, I dunno, I suppose it just really brought up what it means to be Australian to people, instead of like federation and stuff.'[4]

So as well as the excitement factor of these conflicts, there's a real patriotism and pride among many students that's connected with learning this history in school. At a senior secondary college in Canberra, Rick thinks that 'You've got to know what the people were fighting for and why they were there.' His classmate Gunita nodded, adding that Australians at war is important because it gives 'A sense of nationalism'. Ryan, a year 12 student on the New South Wales Central Coast, also explicitly identified with Australia's military past. 'Gallipoli was a defining moment in our history,' he said in his interview. 'I know it sounds clichéd, but we need to develop a sense of who we are. It's important to know what our heritage was.'[5]

These school students reveal a profound sense of connection to Australia's wartime experience. They explain their understanding of 'being Australian' as inextricably linked to a national character that was forged at the beaches of Gallipoli and the trenches of the Western Front. At times during their interviews I couldn't help but feel a little uneasy with this. I'm not suggesting that students' deep connection with the Anzac story isn't heartfelt or genuine, and I was certainly struck by the strength of their identification. But I did wonder whether their belief in Anzac was more like a form of national spiritualism than historical understanding.

I got a similar sense of this national sentiment while reading Bruce Scates' study of pilgrimages to Australian war sites. Scates followed a group of Queensland school students on a trip to Gallipoli and the Western Front in 2002 as part of his research, and used their journals to examine the ways young Australians relate to these historic sites and national commemorations. Dave, a student on the trip, wrote that he'd learnt about Gallipoli since primary school: 'To me, it's the Australian Mecca, a place where we can reflect upon ourselves and what it means to be Australian.'[6] His comments mirror those of many students I spoke with: their own personal interest in Australia's war history is indistinguishable from the collective sense of national identity it evokes.

In fact, I've been surprised by just *how many* students assume this militarised national identity as intrinsically Australian. At a Catholic boys' school in Brisbane, Brendan says that it's important to learn this history because 'Australian identity comes out during the war. The whole mateship sort of thing.' At a boys' school in Adelaide Declan talks about his connection in similar terms: 'Most people say that you shape the country with the way you fight your battles and what comes from that. People are always talking about Australia's freedom is because we fought at Gallipoli and World War II.' He also wondered whether it was a topic that more boys than girls would connect with: 'I don't know, maybe it's just boys and guns, and we could kind of relate to it as eighteen-year-old guys going to war for the country.'⁷

But it isn't just boys who speak with such reverence. Morgan, who goes to a girls' school in Canberra, says that learning about Australians at war 'makes us appreciate, like, the Anzac spirit and everything that we celebrate about it and our nation, because it was our birth as a nation, as people say. It's just so important.' And when I asked a group of year 10 students from a public school in Hobart whether they enjoyed learning about Australia's war history, it was the girls who spoke up first. Julia said she liked the topic 'because they're fighting for *us*. If they weren't fighting Gallipoli, we wouldn't be where we are today.' At another Hobart school, the girls were just as positive. According to Allie, 'our culture is really shaped by that [the wars]. Even though it seems a long time ago, you can relate certain aspects of the Anzac Legend today.' Her classmate Deslie agreed: 'Like the whole "mateship" and everything, it's so Aussie.'⁸

Such expressions of pride certainly weren't universal among all the students I spoke with, but the strength of their identification was undeniable. Not so long ago Anzac Day was thought to be in decline in Australia, and some teachers and curriculum officials were confounded by its currency and appeal. When I asked Greg, a teacher at an independent girls' school in Brisbane, whether he thought students enjoy learning about Australia's military history, he was absolute: 'I think they do more than ever!' he exclaimed. 'I don't know what's happened there. There's this real interest in it. It's gone through the roof lately.' Michael, who works at a rural high school in southern New South Wales, said that it's 'amazing how the kids get involved' at his school's Anzac service. He couldn't believe that 'these rotten little beggars' stay silent for a minute and that so many of them 'go to Anzac Day [services] all across the country'.⁹

John Firth, the Chief Executive Officer of the Victorian Curriculum and Assessment Authority, was also taken by this youthful patriotic pride in the past: 'I'm old enough to remember when Anzac Day was almost moribund,' he said. 'And to see the resurgence around that over the last ten or fifteen years in particular, and the identification of young people with it – there's something going on in the culture there which is interesting, you know.'[10]

So this isn't simply a classroom phenomenon. The allure of Anzac seems to be a growing focus for national identity in Australia more broadly. Numbers at Anzac Day services quadrupled from 1984 to 1995 (increasing from around 50 000 to 200 000), and research into public attitudes towards Australian history confirms this growing patriotic interest. The *Australians and the Past* study conducted by Paula Hamilton and Paul Ashton involved interviews with hundreds of people from around the country who believe Anzac Day is Australia's main patriotic anniversary: it was mentioned by respondents around three times as often as Australia Day or other anniversaries. As the event itself recedes further into the past, the Anzac Legend is becoming an increasingly prominent focus of national commemoration.[11]

Successive governments have certainly helped forge the Anzac hero's mythic status today: Prime Minister Bob Hawke visited Gallipoli in 1990 for the seventy-fifth anniversary celebrations; Paul Keating used equally powerful references to the past in parliament in 1992 when he famously decried the fall of Singapore and later laid to rest the Unknown Soldier at the Australian War Memorial in Canberra; and John Howard even more forcefully recast the 'digger' at the centre of Australia's national identity. It's clear that irrespective of party politics, Anzac Day is 'good' politics – it's a powerful public commemoration where national myth and Australian history have become inextricably entwined.[12]

But back in the classroom, not everyone I spoke with seems equally taken by this growing Anzac affection. In fact, some teachers were quietly cynical about the availability of resources and political support for all things Anzac, and they speculated on the motives behind such intervention. Stephen, who teaches at a Catholic boys' school in Adelaide, said that the topics on war are very well resourced and 'classroom friendly'. But he also wondered if there isn't something more politically motivated behind this growing phenomenon: 'I think there's probably a political agenda running along with that as well.' Elouise from Perth expressed similar thoughts in her interview: 'Well I have a nasty suspicion there's a political agenda in that, and it seems like the only area that there is endless funding for is if it's anything to do with war.'[13]

Anzac history certainly generates more education funding than other areas of Australia's past. There is a wealth of teaching resources, such as those produced by the Department of Veterans' Affairs. There are also individual state prizes for school students, like the Spirit of Anzac prize in Victoria. And then there's the Simpson Prize, a national history award funded by the federal government (and administered by the History Teachers' Association of Australia), which offers a trip to the Anzac Day service at Gallipoli or the Western Front for winners in each state and territory. In 2007, students were asked to 'Consider what values and characteristics demonstrated by the ANZACs at Gallipoli and later reinforced at the Western Front, continue to influence Australians today.' And thousands of them from around the country did just that.

It's difficult to separate the politics from this growing public interest and investment in Australia's Anzac history. Despite the concerns expressed by a few teachers about the political support of Australia's military history and identity, other teachers and students proudly identified with its legacy. Like many Australians, they genuinely connect with the national story it represents – and my own concerns about this Anzac affection certainly *weren't* shared by all those I spoke with.

If anything, this popular belief in the Anzac story is getting stronger. Michael from New South Wales described the importance of studying Australians at war in terms of national pride:

> *I think it's important for them. I think it's part of the Australian image, as sort of pride in yourself, a form of nationalism. ... I certainly oppose jingoism, and I hate the idea of trying to bring back saluting the flag in the school, which we had for a while (I think that's detrimental), but nationalism in the sense of having pride in your people and what's been done, of course.*[14]

A history teacher from a public school in outer Melbourne says the topic is also a vital part of their school calendar. The veterans have 'a ceremony here every year', explains Marco, 'and, you know, the kids love all that sort of stuff and they do need to know that. And especially with our kids from other cultures too, I think as part of the Australian, you know, experience.' Another teacher from Hobart says her students enjoy learning about 'the stories of the individual soldiers, the individual legends, like Simpson and his donkey and so on'.[15]

Anzac Day fulfils a vital role in contemporary Australian society. Rituals such as these surely give meaning and enrichment to our collective national identity, and secular national icons like the Anzac heroes connect us with the nation through its history. When I interviewed a group of students at an independent girls' school in Perth, they explicitly tied the importance of the Anzac story to themselves individually, and to the nation:

> *Do you think it's important to learn about Australians at war?*
>
> **Amanda:** *Yeah, I think it's good to learn like how we get all our mateship.*
>
> **Megan:** *It's like a real Aussie tradition kind of thing.*
>
> **Amanda:** *It's sort of where we got our identity.*[16]

While federation is dismissed by students for being too remote, if anything the Anzac story suffers from the opposite extreme: proximity. Federation may be associated with recounting prime ministers and constitutional conventions in class, but Anzac Day and its heroic legacy continue to live on with increasing popular and political support.

Just because many students identify with this military history, and sometimes quite passionately, I'm not so sure that equates to critical engagement. If the Anzac story does indeed get students interested in Australia's past then we need it more than ever – but that identification mustn't be at the expense of learning history in all its complexity. Historical understanding requires a degree of compassion and identification with the past, but it also demands that critical questions be asked of it: What is the Anzac story? How much is myth and how much history? Can all Australians be Anzacs? Such questions aren't about demolishing the past, or demonising it, but they are a prerequisite for a critical reflection on what it represents.

Simpson and his values

The limitations of understanding the Anzac story as contiguous with our own were made clear in the debate over Australian values a few years ago. In January 2004, Prime Minister Howard said he was concerned about the way he felt values were being taught (or rather *not* taught) in Australian schools. In particular, he criticised public schools for being 'too politically correct and too values neutral'. And he claimed that parents were taking their children out of state school systems around the country because they failed to promote 'mainstream' Australian values.[17]

But what are mainstream Australian values, exactly, and how do they fit into schools? The acting Minister for Education, Peter McGauran, explained the Government's position. 'There is a growing trend that is discernible to parents that too many government schools are either value-free, or are hostile or apathetic to Australian heritage and values,' he said. 'Parents, a great many of them, are worried by a trend within some government schools away from the values that they want imparted to their children.'[18]

Six months later the federal government released the National Framework for Values Education as a response to this apparent dearth in Australian schools. In a joint media release, Prime Minister Howard and the federal Minister for Education, Brendan Nelson, announced a new $31 billion federal education package over four years, which tied government funding to the values framework. This meant that any increased government support would be contingent on the implementation of several policy initiatives in schools, such as the provision of two hours of compulsory exercise for students every week, adopting the national safe schools framework and installing a 'functioning flag pole' to fly the Australian flag.[19]

The flagpole was a clincher for generating debate, and the public was immediately and profoundly divided on the issue. Contributing to an ABC online forum, 'ACT_Hugh' wrote that 'young Australians need to have more patriotism and need to know more about their country, starting with things as basic as our national flag and our national anthem'. Another comment, from 'proud2baussie', also backed the initiative: 'to dismiss this great idea is moronic. I totally support the concept and am proud to be Australian and show our symbols with pride.'[20]

Others weren't so convinced. In a letter to *The Age*, Adrian Wilson gave an unfavourable assessment: 'Schools to salute the flag to get government money!', he quipped. 'Can we now buy national pride?' Polly Price wrote into the *Sydney Morning Herald* and suggested that the Prime Minister 'make the overweight kids shin up the flagpole daily. That should do it.' Matthew Pinkney was just as critical in the *Herald-Sun*: 'It's hard to imagine even Mr Howard could argue a causal link between being forced to raise a flag under pain of financial punishment and the values of citizenry, loyalty and patriotism.'[21]

But flagpoles weren't the only Australian symbol taking up media space in this debate. The government's release of the values themselves was just as contentious. Following the London terrorist bombings in 2005, Brendan Nelson re-launched the values framework, and explicitly linked Australia's values with the Anzac story. Here, this public debate over national values ties in with some of the issues that emerged from my interviews.

Nelson designed a poster of the values 'and over the top of it,' he said, 'I've superimposed Simpson and his donkey as an example of what's at the heart of our national sense of emerging identity.' The story of the unarmed digger and his donkey rescuing wounded soldiers at Gallipoli was the essence of our national character, said Nelson, 'and he represents everything that's at the heart of what it means to be an Australian'.[22]

It wasn't the sentiment of the framework that was controversial. Its nine values – care and compassion, doing your best, fair go, freedom, honesty and trustworthiness, integrity, respect, responsibility, and understanding, tolerance and inclusion – are, I think, genuine. (And I can attest that the posters have been hung in school foyers and principals' offices around the country.) The problem seemed to be that they were tied to government funding and, moreover, tied to a political campaign to define Australia's national character.

Nelson's invocation of Simpson reflected the opinions of many students I spoke with. At a public high school in Darwin, a group of year 12 students considered their study of Australian war history. 'I remember doing a massive thing about Anzac,' Tani said. Adrian remembered learning about 'Simpson and his donkey', before Tani piped up again: 'You just empathise so much,' she said. 'We've learnt heaps about it and I always found it really interesting.'[23] Over in Perth, a group of year 10 students at an independent girls' school spoke about their connection to the Anzac story in similar terms:

> *Do you think it's important to learn about Australians at war?*
>
> **Megan:** *All the Anzacs were concerned it would be a dying tradition but I think it's sort of been kept alive.*
>
> **Jennifer:** *Now they're having like record numbers, and like huge ceremonies all over Australia, and they're like young people that respect it.*
>
> **Sophie:** *And that's good because when you hear about it, especially when you're little and you don't really care and stuff, and they're like, 'Oh, they died for Australia', and you're like, 'Yeah, whatever'. But then you learn about it and what they did do and how they were really heroic and stuff, and you like realise how hard it was.*[24]

It would be naive to dismiss cynically their historical connection with the Anzacs as the simple result of conservative political strategy. Many Australians feel strongly that the nation's past should be 'a source of pride', as former Prime Minister Howard himself articulated. But when the values framework was relaunched by Nelson, Australia's identity was portrayed in very exclusive terms. Nelson reminded his constituents that if they didn't agree with the national character espoused by Simpson (or his donkey), they should reconsider their place in Australian society. 'If you want to be in Australia, if you want to raise your children in Australia, we fully expect those children to be taught and to accept Australian values and beliefs,' Nelson insisted. 'We want them to understand our history and our culture, the extent to which we believe in mateship and giving another person a hand up and a fair go. And basically, if people don't want to be Australians and they don't want to live by Australian values and understand them, well basically they can clear off.'[25]

It was certainly an unfortunate use of 'we' and 'them' to describe the importance of values such as giving everyone a 'fair go' and showing 'understanding, tolerance and inclusion'. Unsurprisingly, given the timing and the tone of his remarks, Muslim schools furiously defended their existing curriculum approaches, and insisted that they already taught Australian values to their students. Silma Ihram, the Principal of the Noor Al Houda Islamic College in Sydney, said that 'Every community has to prove their value to Australian society and our students are doing that.' Speaking on ABC radio's 'The World Today', Iqbal Patel, president of an Islamic school in Canberra, agreed: 'We have in all our schools the very ethos of Australian education, namely respect for each other, mateship, although that's a much-used word in the last few weeks. And you know, teaching the national anthem, flying the flag, teaching "Waltzing Matilda".'[26]

The issue isn't with the values themselves, then, for their sentiments are undoubtedly worthy and genuine. The danger comes when any other interpretation is deemed unacceptable, or worse, 'unAustralian'. In their interviews some teachers also expressed concern about how these Australian icons should be presented to their students. Elouise in Perth cringed when she described how some of her students talked about World War I as if 'Gallipoli is the only thing that exists'. 'It's the only knowledge that they have,' she said, 'and they think it was only Australians.'[27]

There is a real pressure for governments and education departments to define Australia's identity and its values to the next generation, but I hope there's still some scope for them to be nutted out in class, rather than simply prescribed. And, perhaps unsurprisingly, some students have said just as much. At a Catholic boys' school in Brisbane, two year 12 students discussed how Australian history shouldn't be told as a simplistic narrative: 'It's very sort of propaganda-ish, isn't it?' asked Brendan. Arthur paused for dramatic effect, then joked, 'They're toying with our minds!'[28]

When I visited an independent girls' school in Canberra, I was also taken by a particular conversation between two girls about the need to learn Australia's war history. Morgan was insistent on its importance. 'I think war defines us,' she said. 'It's just part of our history and we need to know it.' Annie wasn't so sure:

> *I kind of think though, not to be completely unpatriotic or whatever, but we have a very American outlook on it. Like when they teach Australian history they're like, 'Oh Australians finally got into the war and we got a chance at the world and blah, blah, blah, blah, blah'. But the actual emphasis of the war was that it started in Europe, so the action was in Europe, and it's involving all the European countries ... I find that Australia's a bit insipid because we are such a*

> minor, insignificant part of the war, as bitter as that sounds.[29]

I was quite struck by the way these girls discussed the influence of war on Australia's national character *themselves*. At times, they were so insistent about presenting their point of view that they seemed to forget I was there altogether.

It's critical that this space the Canberra girls had for discussion is preserved, that any effort to promote Australian values doesn't preclude debate about them in class. In other words, it's not the teaching of values to Australian children that is problematic, or even the pride that so many of them obviously have in their heroic representation. The limitation stems from whether these ideas tend to lock in an exclusive understanding of Australian history and identity, or whether they can be launching pads for their very discussion in class. Legends such as Simpson and his donkey may have helped galvanise public interest in the Anzac story. But unless there is space for these figures to be critically analysed in class, there's a risk they will come to represent a very narrow interpretation of Australia's past.

Taking the critique to the classroom

So how do you create and maintain this sort of space for discussion? How do you enshrine not simply Australia's values, but ways for them to be examined in class? Ophelia, who goes to school in Adelaide, explained how she had enjoyed being able to critique and discuss the significance of Australia's Anzac heroes. 'I think for me what was interesting was we got onto Australian identity,' she said. 'And, because everyone's like, "Oh yeah, the digger, that is a true Australian", we sort of went through and decided if we agreed with the principles that everyone thinks what an Australian is.'[30]

While some students' connection with the Anzac story revealed an emotive national pride in the past, Ophelia's engagement offered more critical reflection. Her interest is characterised by discussion and critique rather than sentiment. At a Catholic boys' school in Perth, Cameron says that's also how he likes to teach his students:

> *I guess we have a look at the importance and significance of Anzac Day in Australian history as well, and we have a look at the contribution of Anzac Day to creating a sense of Australian identity. At the same time we also challenge the issue of Anzac Day and we get them to really analyse it and not just have a look at what the media would like us to think about Anzac Day. I guess we get them to have a look at Anzac Day and get them to say well 'Was it important creating an Anzac Legend or was Anzac Day really the Anzac Myth?' So that's what we get them to have a look at.*[31]

Teachers like Cameron don't demand a rejection of the Anzac Legend, or suggest that students shouldn't feel connected to the national identity he has come to represent. Like them, I don't see a problem with students' veneration of the legend, so long as it doesn't exclude other points of view.

In fact, several teachers explained how they try to achieve this 'balance' in their history classes. At a public high school in Adelaide, Lara says that she always teaches about Australia's war history 'and the students enjoy it', but 'I won't teach it as a wonderful promotion of the Anzac Legend,' she adds. 'I mean, that is part of it and it shaped our national identity, but there are parts of that national identity that are not all that great, you know, there's negative and positive aspects, and I would always teach a balance in my class.' Andrew, a teacher at an independent school in Hobart talked about his teaching in similar terms: 'we give them a balanced view,' he said. 'We like to think it's a very balanced view rather than geared towards one side.'[32]

That doesn't mean the Anzac story isn't important to learn, however. 'Of course it's important,' exclaims Tanya, a history teacher near Darwin. 'I mean the whole Anzac myth and Anzac Legend needs to be explained to them, especially when teaching them history, you're also making relevant links to the present and why we're here.' Greg, who teaches at an independent girls' school in Brisbane, also thinks it's important to teach, 'because one way or another,' he reckons, 'militarism has had a place in Australian society.' 'Now, I don't mean that necessarily negatively,' Greg continued, 'because some of the stories of heroism and mateship and egalitarianism grow out of the trenches at Gallipoli, and activities in World War I and World War II, and they form I think what we'd call the "Australian character". So for that reason they're very significant.'[33]

It isn't just teachers who reflect positively on this more complex approach to the past. One of Greg's students, Jiang, enjoyed studying Australians at war because 'there are a lot of different perspectives from which you can actually look at it'. Like Ophelia in Adelaide, she appreciated the different points of view her teacher brought to the topic. In 'primary school they tell you, "This is what happened, this is what our men were like, and this is just the basic idea". Whereas now it's like, "Did this really happen?" and just the whole critical thinking thing that's been incorporated.' Lily agreed: 'I think that in primary school we did the same thing, but this year we've sort of branched out a lot, and looked at it in a lot more detail.' In particular, she liked looking at 'Australia's kind of position on the global scale with all the alliances and all that'.[34]

In other words, lots of kids don't want a parochial Anzac story. And indeed many of them enjoy studying Australians at war precisely because of its broader historical lens. At an independent girls' school in Canberra, Felicity explained that she didn't like learning history in years 9 and 10 so much because it was 'only really the Australian side'. It was 'just such a one-sided thing,' she said. 'Whereas in year 11 and 12 you're looking at every perspective.'[35]

Learning about this international dimension was what made Australians at war so interesting for these year 10 students at an Islamic school in western Sydney. Ramah found Australians at war 'one of the *best* subjects, because it's not just related to Australia, it's international'. Her classmate Yasmin agreed: 'I think it's good because it's at an international level. It's broadening the history which has actually just been limited to Australia.'[36]

Students are genuinely interested in Australia's place in the world, and war history offers a global perspective on the nation's past. Janine Giles, a history teacher who also works for the Curriculum Council in Western Australia, says 'it's all very well for us to say that all students must have some Australian history, but they also have to have other history to put it into context. I mean, it's all very well to talk about the Anzac Legend, but why on earth were we in World War I? What was happening in the rest of the world to make that the case?'[37]

Some students objected to any connection of Anzac with nationalism altogether. At a public senior school in Perth, Maddison said that he didn't enjoy learning the topic 'because it was all the "shaping of the Australian spirit", and it just didn't make any sense to me'. His classmate Hugh expressed similar sentiments: 'I think it's quite hard for our generation to see Australians as being shaped by war, because we've never really lived through a war, and we don't identify Australians as people who have been shaped by war. But we're constantly told that we are and it's a bit hard to actually comprehend.'[38]

At a public school on the New South Wales Central Coast, students were also mixed in their response:

> *Have you ever studied Australians at war?*
>
> **Jill:** *We're doing that now in year 9.*
>
> **Caleb:** *I've found that Gallipoli is really glorified in the course.*
>
> **Ryan:** *It does get a bit more kind of clarified in the higher years in the course that we're doing now.*
>
> **Les:** *The compulsory course is a bit of a one-sided topic.*
>
> **Cate:** *It's very Australian.*
>
> **Caleb:** *Yeah, it's very, very Australian, which is fair enough, because we're learning Australian history, but you've also got to have the other side because war is not one side – especially in the case of the First World War. It wasn't our war. Europe started it, and if you don't learn the European background of it, you've got no real knowledge about Australia's involvement.*[39]

While Caleb, Cate and Les think their history course is narrowly Australian in its focus, Ryan has enjoyed studying the topic, and thinks it has become more 'clarified' in senior years. As they continued their discussion it became clear that they wouldn't come to a defining image of Australia's identity – nor should they be forced to. It was great to see how this group was able to disagree, to debate, and to work out their own positions in class.

And that's exactly what many teachers say too. Jessica, a teacher at a public high school in suburban Brisbane, explains that kids are naturally connected to Australia's military history, but they can respond even better when they're critically engaged. She says students are 'often happy to be engaged with' Australians at war because these historical periods are 'also points of contrast, ... which kids often hold onto in terms of differing opinions and how things are represented differently by different sources'.[40]

When the former president of the History Teachers' Association of Western Australia, Jan Bishop, reflected on what her students had enjoyed most about Australian history, she said they tended to remember the questions it raised in class. They would often say things like 'Well look, we thought it was going to be boring, but we actually liked that bit about conscription and we liked the debate we had about the Anzac Legend, was it a myth or not?'[41]

Many Australians believe history should be a source of pride, and that kids should have an affirming national story with appropriate heroes and values to aspire to. But are we actually any closer to defining what it means to be 'Australian'? The Anzac revival has clearly resonated with many students. It's a heroic Australian story that people can connect with, and they seem to be doing so in droves. The problem is that not everyone feels the same. Despite this groundswell of public and political interest in the Anzac story, a number of historians, teachers and even students worry about cultivating a pride in our national past that's automatic rather than analysed.

As kids flock to honour Australia's wartime history, their growing commemoration of the Anzac Legend in the classroom needs to be accommodated – but it needs to be done so that their historical understanding is expanded rather than limited to any simplistic or uncontested national narrative, especially when so many students are interested in Australia's place in the world. This doesn't mean we should reject icons such as the Anzacs, for they are powerful markers in Australia's past. But we do require space for these national narratives to be discussed critically in class. So long as there's social and political pressure to define our national character, surely the best way for students to deal with contrasting ideas about Australian history and identity is to bring the discussion into the classroom. That way they can actually *contribute* to the debate itself.

CHAPTER 3

1788 and all that

> *Was there any aspect of Indigenous history that you found particularly interesting?*
>
> **Lydia:** *What was it? That agreement, um, was it Mambo? Something like that.*
>
> **Ophelia:** *Mabo!*
>
> **Sam:** *Mambo's a surfwear company.*
>
> **Lydia:** *I was trying to remember it! Yeah, I was really shocked by how the white people didn't accept that the Aboriginals owned the land.*
>
> Year 11 students, co-educational independent school, Adelaide

'... just a little bit of history repeating'

A university tutor once told me that you've probably done enough research for an essay when you start second guessing what scholars are going to say on the topic. Then it's time 'to stop reading and start writing'. In qualitative research this is sometimes called 'saturation' – it's when your respondents begin to answer questions in clear and consistent ways that confirm what you've already been told.

Long before these interviews were finished I had well and truly reached saturation when it came to students' views about learning Indigenous history in school. Of course, they weren't all *exactly* the same. A few students quite liked the topic, while others simply weren't that interested in any history at all, let alone Australia's. Nevertheless, the consistent line from these kids was pretty dismissive: even when they acknowledged the importance of Indigenous history, their experiences have been for the most part boring and repetitive. They've simply been turned off.

To be honest, their views came as a bit of a surprise. Indigenous issues still make headlines in Australia, the history of race relations continues to be at the fore of public debate, and if anything, we're as far from reconciliation in any sense of the word as ever – although, maybe that stasis is precisely what kids are reacting against. I was quite shocked by the negative comments students made about studying Indigenous history. The topic is so politically contentious and raises such important moral questions about how we relate to the past that I thought they would find it absorbing and complex. I couldn't have been further from the mark.

Teachers were the first to speak about this lack of student engagement. Marco says that students at his public school in outer Melbourne aren't afraid to voice their opposition to Indigenous history: 'even my year 12 students, when I say we're doing the first study dot point about early settlement and a lot about Indigenous history, they'll say "Oh, we've done it before, we've done that before".' When Deborah mentions Indigenous history to students at her public senior college in Canberra they moan, 'Oh, not what we did in high school – we looked at Aboriginal lifestyle *forever*.'[1]

In schools around the country, students describe being 'over' Indigenous history. Emma from Hobart reckons some bits 'were interesting but some were really boring'. 'I can't actually remember what was boring,' she says, 'I just remember being bored out of my brains.' Sophia, a year 12 student at a public school in Adelaide, complains that Indigenous history was repeated endlessly in her early years: 'like I did it all the way through primary school, and you kind of learn the same thing again and again and again.'[2]

If their comments seem repetitive, that's because their experiences with the topic are too. At a public high school in Brisbane, Kai complained that Indigenous history 'was like repetitive and boring'. His classmate Trace had the same experience: 'Yeah, we just learnt the same thing every year. It wasn't very interesting.'[3] They were just as exasperated at another Brisbane school:

> *Have you ever studied Indigenous history?*
> **All:** *Yes.*
> **Zach:** *Every year!*
> **Miranda:** *Every year. It's always the same stuff too.*[4]

The experience isn't restricted to state schools. Students from an independent girls' school in Brisbane also criticised the blandness of what they had been taught:

> **Erica:** *I reckon in primary school you got a lot of repetition. Every year you went over the same unit of 'this is like clapping sticks' and 'this is a didgeridoo', and that got a bit tiresome.*
>
> **Jiang:** *I think we've also started to think of Aboriginal history as this sort of one-faceted kind of thing. Like we didn't learn a lot about them other than the fact that, you know, they played didgeridoos, they danced, and this is like the kangaroo dance. We didn't learn much else than that in primary school.*
>
> **Erica:** *Yeah, it was very narrow.*[5]

At a girls' school in Perth, Megan's response was pretty much the same. 'It was the same stuff like over and over again,' she says, 'like, "What hunting tools do they use?" and "What are the common tribes?" and blah, blah, blah – it's so grrrr.'[6]

So it isn't just repetition that's turning students off the topic, but the superficial way they feel it's presented. This history's taught to death, but not *in depth*. Miranda from Brisbane says that 'when we did it in primary school, like we just did the same stuff every year. It was kind of boring, because we just did the same thing over and over again.' Her classmate Chloe was even more critical. 'I don't remember going in depth into it,' she said, 'we only just mentioned it. Like we studied white Australian history a lot more in depth than Aboriginal history. With Aboriginal we just looked at Dreamtime stories, and that's all.'[7]

These kids' experiences aren't all that different to my own. I remember being taught how to decorate postage tubes with dot paintings and then blowing into them in class – we had a cardboard chorus of didgeridoos all right, but it was hardly history. For today's cohort it seems like much of the same. They have a lot of exposure to Indigenous history and culture in school, 'but it's never the nitty gritty stuff,' says Natalie, a year 12 student from Darwin. And in South Australia, while Australian Studies is a compulsory subject for year 11 students, they mainly just studied the 'cultural aspects' of Indigenous history, says Declan, 'like what sports they played and some of their Dreaming stories'. In Brisbane, Trace says that Indigenous history 'was just very marginalised. We didn't do a whole lot of other things that we could have known about. We only were taught certain parts about it and stuff.'[8]

We've ended up with a troubling contradiction. Students complain that they've 'done' Indigenous history and culture – and they've clearly studied it all the way through school – but their actual knowledge is only patchy at best. Tamsyn thinks that students at her Canberra public school simply don't know enough about the very history they complain of: 'they do say "Oh we've *done* this before", but they haven't done it at the depth they need to.' In Adelaide, Lara admits that there's often only a 'smattering' of knowledge among her students. 'You don't know how much they've done and how much they haven't,' she says. Ultimately, says Sarah, who teaches at an independent girls' school in Melbourne, 'it really does need to be taught strategically, and I think that often it's taught not very well, perhaps with not very good resources'. This means that it's 'taught and retaught, perhaps done too much at primary school and then the interest wanes by secondary school and that's a problem'.[9]

Students, too, complained about these poorly co-ordinated curricula. When I asked Les, a year 10 student at a public school on the New South Wales Central Coast, whether he thinks learning about Indigenous history is important, he said, 'Yes, very much so. Although at the moment we learn it bang, bang, bang in year 7, 8, 9 and 10, but too sporadically. It needs to be comprehensive.'[10]

Some teachers even begin the topic by stealth so as to outflank their students' disinterest. Brian, who teaches at Les's school on the Central Coast, tries not to introduce Indigenous history before 'teaching American Indians,' he says. Then 'they think, "It's not right, it's not fair". But if you just come in cold with Aboriginal history a lot of kids will say, "Oh, we've done it in primary school".' In Brisbane, Mary's kids are just as dismissive. 'I mean if you said, "I'm doing Aboriginal stuff", you're going to get a wave of "ugggghhhhhh". If you were to have said you're going to do the same concepts but call it American Negroes, they'd be really interested.' Unfortunately, 'familiarity breeds contempt,' she says. 'They think they know it all therefore they don't want to know any more. And you can be sympathetic to the outsider in someone else's culture. It's much harder to be sympathetic to the outsider when it's your own culture.'[11]

This is a bad situation. Lots of kids have been taught lots of Indigenous content, but it was much harder than I expected to find students who really engaged with it. In fact, the negative responses to Indigenous history were so pervasive that some Indigenous kids I spoke with clearly didn't want to talk about the topic or their attitudes to it in front of their classmates. And a couple even said they didn't think it was particularly important to learn about – I suspect they can't bear to be seen as the 'Indigenous spokesperson' for their class.

This general sense of disinterest was compounded by a number of students who rejected Indigenous history altogether. And it's worrying that their outright refusal to connect with this history is somehow legitimated by the excessive repetition and poor co-ordination of Indigenous material in schools. I was shocked by how fiercely some kids reacted to this topic.

Samantha's response was probably the most extreme. She goes to an independent girls' school in Melbourne and complained that '"invasion" is a guilt trip' teachers pull on their students. 'Like we're meant to feel that our ancestors came and like killed *a billion* Aborigines,' she said, 'and took over a country and gave them diseases.' I couldn't quite believe what I was hearing. Where was this coming from? 'It's kind of bad enough that we're the convict country,' Samantha continued, 'but then when it's drilled into us that we killed everything good in this country, it's like *not fun*.'[12] Not everyone shared her views, of course. Samantha's classmate Leigh spoke up and said she thought non-Indigenous Australians *were* responsible for Indigenous dispossession. But the point had been made: a number of kids don't want to feel 'guilty' for the past, and they're not afraid to say so.

Some of the teachers also picked up on this apparent backlash. Neil, who works at a senior secondary college in Canberra, said that in preparing for our interview he talked to a year 12 student who said 'she'd had a teacher in high school for two years and all they'd had banged into them was the black armband view, and "woe is us", and "we're all bastards" and all that, and she'd found it a real turn off'. This student is a 'politically aware, intelligent lass,' Neil said, 'and if she's finding it a turn off, most kids are probably going to find it a turn off. I think there's too much ideology around it.'[13]

Neil saw his student's reaction as part of a larger shift in historical consciousness in Australia. 'I think kids *hate* being told the "black armband" view,' he said. 'They don't like being made to feel guilty for something that they didn't have any control over.' Other teachers made similar connections. Like Neil, Elizabeth (a former Canberra teacher) says her students didn't want to feel responsible for Australia's colonial history. 'I think also some of them,' she says, 'depending on how it's taught and so on, have a sense of guilt, and "This is meant to make us feel bad".'[14]

This isn't simply the view of students. I suspect many of them have picked up on shifting public attitudes towards Indigenous people and their history more broadly in the last decade or so. Following the election of the Coalition Government in 1996 there was a conscious reconsideration of Australian history. When the Prime Minister said to parliament soon after his election that he believed 'the balance sheet of Australian history is a very generous and benign one', he was marking out a new political direction for Australia's past. In his Menzies lecture later that year, John Howard elaborated on his historical alignment. 'Australian history should never be a source of smug delusions or comfortable superiority,' he acknowledged. 'But nor should it be a basis for obsessive and consuming national guilt and shame.'[15]

Are these students part of Howard's historical generation? Do their values reflect that changing public identification with the nation's history, its Indigenous history in particular? Adrian, a year 12 student in Brisbane, was certainly pretty happy to count himself in. '*We* didn't do it,' he says. 'That's why John Howard refuses to say sorry, because we didn't do anything wrong.'[16]

Of course it's much more complex than simply a question of political leadership. As Judith Brett has convincingly argued, Howard's historical reading surely *responded* to the views of 'mainstream Australia' as much as it helped define them.[17] We have witnessed a real turning point in public debates over Australia's historical values, where anything overtly critical has been labelled 'black armband' and any assertion of historical guilt quickly dismissed.

But this isn't just a case of politics in the classroom. While the conservative political refusal to say 'sorry' for Australia's historical wrongs may have contributed to students' discontent, this has been more than matched by a lack of curriculum organisation and support. Kids repeatedly say they're bored with Indigenous history, and it's troubling that rejections of 'guilt' like Samantha's or Adrian's are somehow legitimated by the repetitive nature of the subject.

It was confronting to see student after student rolling their eyes when asked about their attitudes to Indigenous history. Somewhat naively, I suppose, I went into the interviews with a clear sense that Indigenous history matters deeply in Australia. If I find it interesting, I reasoned, shouldn't they? But many students had already turned off.

The curse of curriculum

So what on earth has gone wrong? Why do so many kids criticise their experiences of learning about Indigenous history, even when they acknowledge it's important to know? Once again, the students themselves offer a clue. *Do you think it's important to learn about Indigenous history today?*, I asked a group of girls at an independent school in Perth:

> Megan: *To an extent, yeah.*
>
> Jennifer: *But not overdo it.*
>
> Sophie: *Yeah, if you overdo it people start to not care.*[18]

I'm confident that most kids haven't yet *stopped* caring about Indigenous issues, and we'll see their views on that later in the chapter. But they're certainly sending out a loud warning about the way they've been taught to date.

Part of the problem could be that Indigenous history teaching doesn't have a long history of its own. Many teachers didn't learn about it themselves at school, and if they did it wasn't a large aspect of their education. A generation ago, Indigenous perspectives were marginal at best, and until waves of new historical writing emerged in the 1960s and 70s, Australian history was relatively untroubled by the questions it posed.

Since then, hundreds of scholars and commentators have worked towards understanding and overturning this exclusion, which they saw as historically limiting and morally suspect. It was, as the anthropologist WEH Stanner famously said in his 1968 Boyer Lectures, our 'Great Australian Silence'. And the efforts of Indigenous and non-Indigenous writers and historians to increasingly fill in this silence by incorporating Indigenous perspectives has greatly changed Australian history over the last few decades.

The rewriting of history syllabuses and teaching documents wasn't far behind the growing reappraisal of Australia's past. In the 1970s and 80s there was a huge shift in history teaching in Australia. Curriculum documents increasingly took Indigenous perspectives into account, state education departments such as New South Wales even enacted their inclusion across all curricula. And if you take the time to look back over the various professional journals of the History Teachers' Associations from around the country during this period, there is a noticeable effort to accommodate the histories of women, migrants and Indigenous people in their teaching practices and approaches.[19]

This inclusion, and even mandating, of Indigenous perspectives fundamentally altered the ways Australian history was conceived and taught in the classroom. In one generation Australian history education underwent a radical reworking, and many of the curriculum designers and teachers I spoke with have personal experience of this reorientation. When I interviewed Julie Fisher, Principal Education Officer for Studies of Society and Environment in the Department of Education in Tasmania, she compared the sort of curriculum she was currently developing with her own history education. 'We need to think about what education should look like in the twenty-first century and it's not the same as what it was for me in my education in the 60s and 70s,' she said. 'In fact,' she continued, 'the Australian history I was taught at school was not an accurate view of history because it did not acknowledge the Indigenous owners of the land.'[20]

In these interviews with teachers and curriculum officials, the ways they talked about learning Indigenous history graphically contrasted with the experiences of their students. While kids around the country lacked interest, their educators had often been quite challenged by their engagement with the topic, and often presented their experiences as a narrative – mirroring Australia's own changing historical appreciation.

Their reflections also reminded me of the historian Henry Reynolds's historical awakening in his autobiography, *Why Weren't We Told?* In the book, Reynolds writes how he became increasingly aware that Indigenous history was an untold piece of Australia's past. 'I felt that my generation of Australians should have been told the truth about the border wars,' he wrote, 'about the pioneers' complicity in murder, abduction and rape; about fear and hatred; about the way Australia was acquired.'[21] The responses of teachers and curriculum designers were often framed in these terms of a growing personal understanding of Indigenous history – it's knowledge that they weren't offered at school, but is now available to their students.

One Indigenous student teacher I spoke with said the fact she was taught so little Indigenous history at school motivated her to become a history teacher. Where Kylie went to school, 'Aboriginal history wasn't being taught,' she said. She was 'the only Aboriginal kid in class in an era when Aboriginal people weren't really part of history'.[22]

In South Australia, Terry Woolley, the Executive Director of Primary, Middle and Senior Secondary Services at the Department of Education and Children's Services, compared the Australian history book he had been given in school (*Australia Since 1606*, by GV Portus) with contemporary historical approaches. It was 'a wonderful little book,' says Woolley, 'and I believed every word of it in year 9 because I had to. Now I should imagine that it would be a jaundiced, narrow, sexist, racist book, without even reading it, and I don't think we should be exposing our kids to that.'[23]

By some coincidence I had been given a copy of the book that morning by a generous teacher in Adelaide who was trying to make the same point. It was a copy from 1955, which by that stage had been reprinted fourteen times since the first edition in 1932. *Australia Since 1606* is the sort of book in which, if you look up 'Aboriginals' in the index, it says '*See* Blacks'. It comes from an era where the extinction of Aboriginal people was thought to be inevitable.[24]

Portus's reading of Indigenous history is precisely what these teachers and curriculum officials are reacting to, and a trope of personal change comes through quite strongly in a number of their interviews. Michael teaches in a country town in southern New South Wales and remembered how little Indigenous history he had been taught. 'The thing that I tell them, and that amazes me, is that in our childhood, we didn't know about any of it,' he says. 'My baby boomer generation didn't know anything about it. Even my grandmother, who was fascinated by Aboriginal things and did a lot for Aboriginal people, she didn't know about the Stolen Generation or whatever.'[25]

Greg, who teaches at an independent girls' school in Brisbane, seemed mortified by his early approach to Australian history. 'And, to my embarrassment, when I started teaching in the 1970s,' he said, 'we didn't, we just didn't teach Aboriginal history. If we did it was boomerangs and woomeras. I would have had Aboriginal kids in my class in those years! So I'm embarrassed that I've ignored students in my class.'[26]

I even wonder whether at some level students' apparent rejection of Indigenous history is also a generational response of sorts. Are kids snubbing these attempts to incorporate Indigenous perspectives because they see their teachers' interest as too worthy, too well meaning, and therefore uncool? Perhaps it's a little like their attitudes to studying federation: because students sense they *should* know about it, because it's a topic that grown-ups deem important and 'politically correct', many of them don't want to know about it.

So unfortunately, while the Great Australian Silence has been significantly challenged in history teaching, this hasn't translated into lasting student engagement at school. This doesn't mean that student attitudes are locked in some intractable resistance to learning Indigenous history. Indeed, it's clear that student attitudes *have* shifted over time. Some teachers noticed that among their students, the appreciation of Indigenous history had come into line with the changing curriculum. Sarah, who teaches at an independent girls' school in Melbourne, says that comments in the classroom had noticeably changed in her time there:

> *I've noticed a real difference in student attitudes over the fifteen years or so that I've been teaching this topic. We have a lot of country girls, boarders, and I used to find that at the beginning of the unit the country girls would be very, very critical of Aboriginal people and as the unit progressed I could really see their attitudes change. Now, those sorts of girls don't express the heavy criticism that they used to have no hesitations about expressing in a classroom.*[27]

But this curriculum reorientation doesn't seem to have been conducted in any coherent manner. And that means that while students are receptive to issues of social justice and acknowledge the importance of including Indigenous perspectives in Australian history, they're not so keen on being taught the same thing over and over again.

In the lead-up to the Coalition government's National History Summit in August 2006, I did some work for a report on the current state of Australian history education from years 3 to 10 in each of the states and territories. The report found that 'there is absolutely no consistency of curriculum approach' around the country. Furthermore, 'there is no guarantee that the vast majority of students in Australian schools will have progressed through a systematic study of Australian history by the end of Year 10,' it stated. 'Indeed, the opposite is almost certainly the case. By the time they reach leaving age, most students in Australian schools will have experienced a fragmented, repetitive and incomplete picture of their national story.'[28]

Comments from students and teachers show quite clearly that this lack of co-ordination is especially true for Indigenous history. Even in New South Wales, where Australian history is mandated in years 9 and 10, there is potential for overlap and repetition. The history curriculum for years 7 and 8, for example, requires students to learn about 'Aboriginal and Indigenous Peoples, Colonisation and Contact History'. Yet in each learning Stage, from kindergarten to year 6, Indigenous content is also required.[29]

Obviously, the objective of curriculum designers and writers is for students' knowledge to grow and develop and deepen over time. The New South Wales syllabus for years 7–10 even states that the 'topic builds upon prior learning of Aboriginal and non-Aboriginal contact history in Stages 1–3 [years K–6]'.[30] This is a significant educational aim for the subject: if historical knowledge is to be more than simply a set of facts, students shouldn't just learn something and then move on to the next topic.

It's also an approach to learning that's characteristic of curriculum frameworks from around the country – even in those states and territories where history is subsumed into interdisciplinary subjects such as Studies of Society and Environment (or SOSE). The Queensland SOSE syllabus from years 1–10 states that 'Because reflective inquiry involves introspection and reconsideration of values, processes and concepts, these phases of inquiry will rarely be followed in strict sequential order but are revisited. In this way, reflective inquiry is phased and recursive.' And in South Australia, outcomes for learning Indigenous history shift only slightly from years 6 to 10 as students build on their existing knowledge.[31] In other words, as the topics recur, students revisit them in different and increasingly complex ways – that's the ideal, at any rate.

In practice, however, it's very hard to organise and maintain a consistent approach to knowledge and learning across the duration of one child's education as they change year levels, teachers and schools. Curriculum frameworks are large and unwieldy documents that contain masses of content, learning outcomes, standards, benchmarks and a maze of cross-referencing. And somewhere in all of that is a plan for every child's education.

Furthermore, because specific content is rarely prescribed in the curriculum frameworks, particularly in primary school, it means that students rarely have the same background knowledge. For example, level 5 (early to middle high school) students in Queensland schools have to demonstrate that they understand 'aspects of diverse cultural groups including Aboriginal and Torres Strait Islander groups'. Suggested topics for achieving the outcome include studying Indigenous 'music, codes and creeds, family structures, gender roles'.[32] Yet none are stipulated.

While the progressive developmental approach is important for giving kids a *deeper* knowledge of certain historical topics, the way it stands now, many don't share the same knowledge. And the most critical disjuncture in curriculum co-ordination occurs between primary and secondary schooling, when that break in schools means curriculum parity is tested even more. There seems to be little co-ordination and consistency between the primary and secondary school sectors in terms of organising the curriculum and then teaching it. And a number of the secondary teachers I spoke with commented about the problems of this apparent blockage. Because nothing is clearly defined, it's unclear what any given student has learnt, let alone a whole cohort.

So instead of an increasingly complex and recursive approach to Indigenous history, we have a repeated approach – and a significant backlash from students. Lee, a year 12 student from Canberra, says that it isn't the topic itself that's the problem, but the way it's organised: 'Well, when you're first taught about Indigenous history it's interesting. But each year, when they teach it again and again, it might lose a bit of interest.'[33]

This doesn't mean the answer is a totally prescribed version of Australian history, where every student should study ten weeks of Indigenous history, written centrally, in year 5 or year 9 or wherever. Of course there should be room for local topics and perspectives – and this tension between the needs of individual classes and the imperative to reduce curriculum repetition is explored in greater detail in the next chapter.

Why would students in Broome have the same connections with Indigenous histories as those in Byron Bay or suburban Melbourne? And of course there should be scope for students' knowledge and understanding of Indigenous history (indeed, history generally) to grow and develop, which by its nature means revisiting certain events over time. But if there's no co-ordination, this case of history repeating will almost certainly continue to alienate students.

'Indigenous history still matters'

Indigenous history is hard to teach well. Even beyond questions of curriculum planning, the massive shift to incorporate Indigenous perspectives brought with it new difficulties for teachers. While the previous exclusion of Indigenous voices and perspectives perpetuated a narrow and limited version of Australian history, its overturning has highlighted questions about historical voice itself – namely, who can tell this story, and how? Some teachers feel reluctant to touch on aspects of Indigenous history because they're not comfortable speaking about someone else's experience.

Neil from Canberra says that 'It's not an area, to be honest, in which I feel particularly confident.' And when he has 'wanted to do anything other than the straight politics of Aboriginal rights in a white society,' he says, 'I've tried to get in Indigenous guest speakers because I feel more comfortable with them telling their own story than me – that's not because I think I don't understand, I just think it's more appropriate.' Teachers worry that by speaking for Aboriginal people, they may in fact be maintaining the very silence they hoped to overturn. But who is able to bring in an Indigenous expert every time the topic is raised? And when they can't, does that mean Indigenous history is off limits?[34]

These aren't easy questions to answer. The inclusion of Indigenous perspectives has fundamentally challenged the way Australian history is approached, and we ignore them at our historical peril. But not to teach it altogether would be even riskier. I suspect the wariness that a number of teachers feel about this topic has contributed to some of the repetition students have experienced. Teachers end up offering what they know, what is safe, simply because there aren't the resources or the possibilities for professional development to do any differently.

This isn't about overcoming some sort of cult of cultural relativism in the classroom, but helping teachers to present this history sensitively and confidently. Indigenous history is difficult to teach because it's a difficult history. The moral questions raised by colonisation, dispossession and even reconciliation aren't easily answered in the courts, let alone the classroom – and this makes support for teachers even more important.

Many teachers, often experienced ones at that, are troubled by the opportunities and resources available to teach Indigenous history to their kids. It means that history lessons often feel too one-sided, says John, who teaches at a public girls' school in Sydney. 'We visit museums, like the city museum, and we have the people talking to them. And we see the artefacts, performances and so forth. But that really sort of is Aboriginality "on show", isn't it, rather than coming to a real understanding.'[35]

Susan, an Indigenous student teacher from New South Wales, was particularly critical of the classroom texts she had had to teach with: 'It's like they don't want to be controversial. The textbooks don't teach all of the story. They're selective in what they teach.' For Tamsyn in Canberra, there are also problems with resources at her school. 'I think we're sometimes strapped for resources,' she says. 'And I've heard kids say, "Oh, we've watched *Rabbit Proof Fence*. We watched in year 6, we watched in English. I don't want to watch this anymore." So you have to be careful about that.'[36]

Even in areas with a high proportion of Indigenous students, it is a contentious and problematic topic – and perhaps its very presence in the classroom makes it all the more difficult to grapple with. At a large public school in central Australia, Justine explained that when she first arrived at the school and taught a unit on the Myall Creek massacre, she thought she'd tie it in to the Coniston massacre, which had occurred locally in 1928, as a way of contextualising the topic. But 'I didn't really realise it was quite as sensitive as that,' she says. There are 'still people around who were babies, young children at that time, and there's still a great deal of disagreement between people around here'. It 'was far too close to home,' she admits, and 'I realised that without knowing I touched on something that I shouldn't have touched on'.[37]

David, who teaches in a small town in central Australia, has also come up against local resistance. 'I tend to stay away from it here in this area because there is, you know, this is fairly local and [there were] a few massacres in this area with some of the local tribes so one has to be careful how you dance.' His position is a tricky one, he says, 'because it's actually considered that most of we white people are considered to be the invaders and we're the ones responsible ... I'm not old enough to have done massacres, but I mean it comes from first encounter times'.[38]

Indigenous history isn't ancient history, as these teachers remind us. It's playing out every day in their classrooms. At a school near Darwin, Tanya says that her kids have a 'very rural mindset'. 'I don't like using the word redneck,' she says, 'but a lot of the kids come from redneck backgrounds and I feel that's in one way why we've steered clear from doing straight units on Indigenous history because there does get a bit of antagonism.' As a teacher, she has to negotiate not only the needs of her Indigenous students but the politics of the area she lives and teaches in, as well as the topic itself: 'We do actually have a high population of Indigenous students here, but if it's taught as Indigenous history, quite a few of the kids get their backs up and [complain] "What are we learning about this for" and blah, blah, blah. So you have to be quite careful.'[39]

Despite these difficulties, however, and despite the endless 'we've done it before' comments from the classroom, teachers and students overwhelmingly identify the need for Indigenous history in school. While they deplore the repetition they've experienced, kids understand its importance in Australian history. Gabby, a year 12 student at a public school in Darwin, said that the previous year their history teacher had 'walked into the room and said that history is so important because you can't understand where you are now or where you want to be in the future if you don't understand what's happened'. While her teacher 'applied that to European history,' Gabby said, 'I think it works even more with local history or Aboriginal history, to understand what's happened in your country in the past.'[40] There is a strong sense in some of the interviews that despite the difficulties of teaching Indigenous history, *not* teaching it would be far, far worse.

Says Mary, a high school teacher in Brisbane, 'I have a five year rule: if I'm selecting things, I want either the content or the process to matter to them in five years, and I think Indigenous history still matters.' Jessica, another Brisbane history teacher, also insists its place is central in the curriculum. 'Indigenous history is obviously an integral element of Australian history, and to deny that is to deny who we are,' she says. 'I think increasingly people have acknowledged that – that it's not a particular perspective. It's simply a dimension of the whole, and it can't be overlooked.'[41]

It isn't just the tangible benefits of knowing this history that drives teachers. For Greg, studying Indigenous history is 'important because it's a brand new perspective. It's a bit like when feminism arrived in the 1970s and gave us a whole new way of looking at previous interpretations,' he continued. 'Well, this is another perspective that gives us new ways of looking at old evidence, so it's exciting for that reason.' Brian also senses the intellectual significance of the topic. 'It's an integral part of understanding who we are,' he says, 'and if history's going to have any role, if studying history in school is to give kids the critical dimension of understanding their society's place in the world, who they are as an individual and at a societal level, then I think it's a really important part of our story.'[42]

While respondents in so many of these interviews expressed frustration at how Indigenous history has been taught, their belief in its presence in history syllabuses has been as strong. And, like their teachers, students consistently acknowledged the need to understand Indigenous history. Sam from Adelaide warned that 'If we didn't have any knowledge of what happened between Europeans and Aboriginals' then Australia would remain divided. 'It would make reconciliation a lot harder if there wasn't any knowledge of the background issues.' At a state high school in Hobart, Tenealle compared her education to that of her parents: 'When our parents [went to school], they didn't learn anything. They learnt that the Aboriginals had all gone, and they didn't really learn anything about what happened to them.' 'Yeah,' agreed her classmate Michelle, 'it's important to know what happened.'[43] In Melbourne, Esme thinks 'it's really important' to learn Indigenous history. 'I mean, I think it's pretty evident that there's still a lot of, you know, non-accepting people in Australia of different cultures.'[44]

These kids believe in the significance of Indigenous history despite the repetitive nature of what they've been taught. In fact, when I asked a group of students in Brisbane whether it was important, they framed their response in these terms precisely – yes it is important, they said, but it has to be better managed:

> **Linda:** *Yeah, I think it's really important, especially Aboriginal history, because that is really our heritage, despite the European colonisation or invasion or whatever.*
>
> **Miranda:** *It's important, but they need to broaden the curriculum in what they teach, instead of just doing the same things.*
>
> **Linda:** *And maybe teach what's happening today, rather than just what happened then, because it's still history.*[45]

It's heartening that students still sense the interest and importance of this topic. They recognise that it offers different perspectives on the past, and it challenges them to think differently. That's certainly what Mal hopes to achieve through his teaching. As an Indigenous history teacher from the Northern Territory, he's a rare voice in all of this, but he says 'the satisfaction I get out of it is when kids walk away and they think, "Oh, I didn't expect to think about those sort of issues".' He teaches Indigenous history so that his students 'can understand some of the issues without a blind, you know, view of things. That's how I want my students to go through, to get that sort of result.'[46]

Yet many students are caught in a mismatch between good intentions and good teaching. Kids want historical complexity that's well planned; they don't want repeated messages, says Ellen, who teaches at a public high school in Darwin: 'They're not interested in hearing this kind of potted version of the Dreamtime and all that sort of rubbish, you know.' Students don't like 'bullshit,' she said. 'I think they like anything that's real and true. But as soon as you start trying to push a line down their throat they get a bit anti.'[47]

Her comments were backed up by a number of students. Annie, for one, explained that she didn't want a simple story of

Indigenous history: 'Like the political struggle for land and that kind of thing is probably more interesting than learning about what they ate, to be honest.' In Hobart, Allie likes it when the teacher can 'question you and you have big class discussions about it'. Ultimately, says Ellen, kids don't want a safe, tired narrative of Indigenous people: 'I think the assumption that kids want some sort of, I don't know, panacea or some sort of an apology – apologist history or something – I think is wrong.'[48]

Beyond their pleas for a more consistent approach to Indigenous history, these interviews also give us a clue as to what kids find interesting about the topic. Far from learning a 'safe, tired narrative', Annie and her Canberra classmates reckon it's the complexity of Indigenous history that has helped them understand its importance:

> Felicity: *Because it makes us respect what has happened here and it makes us respect what the Aboriginals went through when Europeans came and how things have changed.*
>
> Annie: *It also allows us to create, um, we're not exactly ignorant anymore and we're able to found our own opinions. Although, of course, sometimes you get in class and it's a little one-sided. Our teacher is really great. She's really open and everything, so we can establish what we really believe and how we feel about the situation.*
>
> Felicity: *Like you can't go through life not knowing that there was people here when the Europeans invaded. Like little kids, they just think, 'Oh yes, that's it, we've been here forever', but the Aboriginals call that Invasion Day.*[49]

So it's the debates about Indigenous history that engage these students, as much as the history itself. That's also how the New South Wales History Extension course approaches the subject. It's aimed at more advanced year 12 history students, and tackles historiographical questions in a way that lets students themselves in on the debates: Why do historians disagree? Why do historical approaches change over time? History Extension covers ancient and modern history, but its units on colonial Australian history are particularly relevant to thinking about how we can engage students in historical discussions like the history wars – for these heated public debates over the past stand in such contrast to the staid, repeated lessons so many of them complain about.[50]

Such an approach doesn't need to be limited to advanced senior students. Questioning students' assumptions and probing their beliefs is exactly how Marco likes to teach his classes in the outer suburbs of Melbourne. Students 'like confronting the stereotypes,' he says. 'When you actually confront the stereotypes with them, you know, their eyes are open to all of that at once, if you can get the right material and the right approaches.' By incorporating current questions and debates, he thinks students get a more developed historical picture that they can really connect with. 'I try to say, "Well, you know, some people say this didn't happen and this didn't happen". I think it's very interesting even for kids to discover it all because, you know, it's a pretty recent phenomenon even though it's just filtering in to schools, I think.'[51]

Students haven't been completely closed off from Indigenous history – it's just that most of them have had very sporadic approaches to the topic, with far too much repetition and not enough material they can engage with. And this means it's just *that much* harder to get them switched on again. Janice admits that her students 'often come initially with, "Oh, not Aboriginal history again". But once they got into it,' she says, they 'saw that we were trying to build' on their previous knowledge. The students got interested because 'we had a slightly different approach, I suppose, a more mature approach than just, you know, "This is the Dreamtime story".'[52]

It's confounding that so many students seem to have had bad experiences learning Indigenous history. For a subject that arouses such heated public debate, kids couldn't be more uninspired by it. But it's also clear from their interviews that they genuinely think Indigenous history is important to understand – and this little window of interest means there's still potential to turn students' attitudes towards the subject around. None of this is easy of course: designing a curriculum is hard; teaching it is even harder. And from experience we can see the tension between encouraging development and depth in historical understanding while also maintaining some sort of coherence in the curriculum. But until that co-ordination is successful, and unless there are additional teaching resources and professional development to generate interested and critical engagement, Indigenous history will remain just as marginalised in schools.

CHAPTER 4

A national curriculum

> *Do you think Australian history should be a compulsory school subject?*
>
> **Pia:** *It already is really – and I heard them talking in the news about that. I think we do it a bit too much. Like we learn about it in primary school – most schools do – and then in younger years at high school you learn about it, but it's basically going over the same thing.*
>
> **Chen:** *Yeah, I think it should be compulsory, like at one stage of your life, but not like throughout your primary school and throughout your high school.*
>
> Year 11 students, public girls' school, Sydney

The renaissance kids

When Prime Minister Howard called for a 'root and branch renewal' of Australian history teaching on the eve of Australia Day in 2006, he said he wanted to restore 'our national sense of self' in schools. Howard insisted that history teaching had come to be dominated by themes and issues, and there wasn't any clear sense of national identity or heritage that students could aspire to. 'In the end,' he warned, 'young people are at risk of being disinherited from their community if that community lacks the courage and confidence to teach its history.'[1]

He had plenty of supporters. *The Australian*'s columnist Janet Albrechtsen backed Howard's history push, arguing that 'there is much work to be done in undoing the progressive curriculum foisted on Australian schoolchildren'. In a similar vein, the educationist Kevin Donnelly thought the Prime Minister's speech anticipated a swing back to a more content-driven approach to history teaching. 'Was John Howard correct this week? Has the teaching of history fallen victim to a politically correct, New Age approach to curriculum, and are students receiving a fragmented understanding of the past?', he asked rhetorically. 'The evidence suggests "yes".'[2]

Some eager letter-writers and bloggers joined the polemicists in backing the Prime Minister. Grattan Wheaton wrote to the Adelaide *Advertiser* and agreed 'with everything Mr Howard said about the teaching of history/geography subjects in schools.' In *The Australian*, Anne-Marie Irwin wanted to 'congratulate John Howard for his Australia Day speech'. 'I believe we are fortunate to have a Prime Minister who is a true statesman, and not merely a politician,' she continued. 'His thoughts regarding the teaching of the humanities and of the need to present a coherent picture to the rising generations in this period of postmodern deconstructionism will strike a chord in the hearts and minds of many teachers.'[3]

This was more than just conservative populism: Howard had tapped into a national concern over history education that went beyond the pages of *The Australian*'s education campaign against progressive 'political correctness'. It wasn't that support for his history revival was across the board, or even that the endorsement he generated was completely unqualified. But there was significant popular approval. Many Australians are worried about what kids know about the past, and Howard's remarks spoke to them especially. Commentators, parents and innumerable 'concerned citizens' quickly acknowledged his call to strengthen the subject in schools, particularly the primacy of the national narrative in affirming Australia's identity and history.

It's not as if this was a bolt out of the blue. The urge to teach 'the Australian Achievement' in schools is a position that many Australians have shared for a long time. They see that the role of history is to educate 'tomorrow's citizens' about their national heritage and identity – it's the conduit for developing knowledge and pride in the nation and its past. Correspondingly, any failure to connect with our national story is seen as a threat to the identity, strength and character of the nation itself. So it's no wonder that so much concern has been generated over surveys revealing a profound ignorance among young people about Australia's past.

Kids aren't immune to this popular pressure to remember the past. When I asked a group of boys at an Islamic school in western Sydney whether Australian history should be a compulsory subject, Oyuz thought it probably should, 'Because it's good to know what happened in the past'. His classmate Ahmed captured the sentiment even more strongly: 'It's not just good to know,' he said, 'we *should* know.'[4] As the anxious discussion about what 'our children' should know continues to play out in the media and in public debate, students themselves certainly sense the importance that many Australians place on national historical knowledge.

It's hardly just an Australian concern. For example, a 1987 report by Chester E Finn and Diane Ravitch in the United States argued that their test results of almost 8000 students revealed a generation 'gravely handicapped' by their own ignorance. After a series of Canadian history surveys conducted by the Dominion Institute in the late 1990s showed a worrying lack of knowledge among Canada's youth, some were prompted to warn that any ignorance of the nation's history could threaten the future of the nation itself. And in 2001, the British *Daily Telegraph* reported significant public concern over results of a survey in which some schoolchildren astonishingly thought Adolf Hitler was Britain's Prime Minister in World War II.[5]

Outrage about the state of historical knowledge appears with predictable regularity: surveys publish damning results about young people's ignorance; politicians, commentators and letter-writers express disbelief that anyone could let it get *that bad*; meanwhile, teachers are left with the same curriculum to teach to the same bunch of kids. As the American history educationist Sam Wineburg wryly noted, 'The whole world has turned upside down in the past eighty years but one thing has seemingly remained the same: Kids don't know history.'[6]

But why such anxiety over history education? Why do headlines proclaiming its demise appear on newspaper front pages year after year? The concern is essentially a national one. As one correspondent lamented to *The Australian* in 2006, if students don't learn about 'our past' then 'we face the tragic reality that our future leaders will have no idea how our nation developed'.[7] There's a widespread belief in the power of history to hold the nation together into the future – hence the pervasive collective pronouns in debates over 'our history'. And there is no more powerful symbol of that future than the very kids who continue to disappoint an anxious public almost annually.

Around the world, various 'history wars' have broken out over museum exhibits, national commemorations and history textbooks. Just think of the disquiet that China expresses every time a Japanese leader visits the Yasukuni war shrine in Tokyo that includes the remains of Japanese soldiers convicted of war crimes, or the question of whether official apologies ought to be made for slaves sold to the Americas or victims of the Holocaust or the Stolen Generations. You don't need a PhD in political science to gauge the depth and power of these debates over the past.

These public debates haven't dented the widespread anxiety over young Australians' historical knowledge because that anxiety is preoccupied with learning core national facts rather than encouraging historical engagement. While politicians, commentators and the general public debate the meaning and importance of Australian history, students themselves don't have a clear sense that being taught more content in a firm national narrative is the answer. These students from a public school near Darwin were far from united on the issue:

> *Do you think Australian history should be a compulsory subject?*
>
> **Keira:** *No. I reckon it should be a subject that's like an elective sort of. Like it's there for people who want to do it, but all the people who hate it don't have to.*
>
> **Simon:** *I reckon some basic history should be compulsory, like Anzac Day and federation and women's rights.*
>
> **Danh:** *Yeah, history is important for the present time.*[8]

Keira doubted the need for any mandatory Australian history because many students (herself included) simply 'hate it'. Meanwhile, Danh and Simon thought that knowledge of Australia's past 'should be compulsory' because it's impossible to understand 'the present time' without it.

Many kids think Australian history is important to know, but they're not so sure how to make the subject relevant for everyone. Alex, a year 12 student from Adelaide, said that it should be compulsory, but 'Not all the way through,' he added. 'Maybe up to year 10 or something, because in year 9 and year 10, I didn't do it then because I knew there were going to be people who didn't want to be there – they'd just be picking it as a bludge subject. And so it's not really good to learn when there's people who don't want to be there.'[9]

Perhaps it's just the 'Edmund Barton syndrome' all over again. While grown-ups endlessly worry about the state of Australian history education, kids are far more likely to choose any subject *other* than Australian history when the decision's up to them. In Victoria alone, year 12 Australian History has been steadily declining in recent years. In 2006 only 1243 students took the subject. Meanwhile, 4832 took the history subject Revolutions, considered to be a more exciting, and bloodier, course. And if you compare this with the 15 203 who chose to study Psychology, you get an even better sense of what students consider relevant and interesting.[10]

But it's figures like these that keep driving the public and political concern over the subject. So when Prime Minister Howard called for a 'root and branch renewal' of Australian history teaching, he wasn't just demanding an educational restoration, but a national one. 'This is about ensuring children are actually taught their national inheritance,' he said.[11] In other words, national pride is impossible without a national history education – it's a type of historical engagement synonymous with national identity itself. And as we saw with some of the responses to Howard's Australia Day address, this stance is shared by many.

Likewise, when the Education Minister Julie Bishop said she wanted to see 'a renaissance of Australian history in our schools', she was also advocating a more coherent and prominent national story. In fact, she went one further, calling together a national history summit of eminent historians, educators and public commentators to develop an Australian history curriculum.[12] 'We have a rich and unique national story,' Bishop affirmed, but 'We have to ask ourselves why so few of our children know it.'[13]

Opening the summit, the Education Minister pushed two government objectives: 'We want to canvass ideas that will strengthen the teaching of history in our schools,' she said; and 'we want to identify the key historical events, facts, dates and details that should be part of this structured narrative.'[14] For the government at least, the summit was a chance to anchor the subject to a set of core national knowledge. By the time they finish their secondary schooling, Bishop insisted, Australian students should 'have a thorough understanding of their nation's past, and how we have become a modern liberal democracy'.[15]

But when it came down to it, the political momentum for a more cohesive and comprehensive story of the 'Australian Achievement' in schools couldn't be sustained at the summit itself. Despite the hopeful editorials, eager correspondence and positive public response to the government's urgings, the day became a forum for 'Australian history' the subject, rather than a declaration of core national knowledge.

The 'summiteers', as they came to be known, didn't rubber stamp the government's prompts for a fact-based narrative approach. All keenly acknowledged the importance of a stronger national history presence in schools, and they agreed with the importance of teaching the facts as part of a comprehensive historical education. But a number of participants were concerned about mandating content at the expense of teaching skills of inquiry and analysis, or the classroom activities that connected students to the subject.

Ultimately, the summit departed from the government's history agenda. The debate over national history education didn't need to be a contest between enjoying history and learning it, participants figured; surely it should aim to be both. And when the history educationist Tony Taylor insisted that any Australian history curriculum had to be 'doable', 'teachable' and 'sustainable', the summit quickly adopted his terms as guiding principles.[16]

This wasn't to say that historical knowledge became sidelined. A working party was drawn from the summit to develop a more coherent national approach to Australian history, and incorporate 'milestones' of Australian history content. But, critically, most summiteers kept returning the discussion to the realities of the classroom, where any government effort to mandate a national narrative made up of key facts and dates was going to have to be realised. In other words, they reasoned, there's no use having a national history course if kids aren't going to learn it.

Between compulsion and revulsion

I went to quite a few schools to research this book, sat in on history classes, and spoke with teachers from around the country. It's them, not the politicians and columnists, who have to front up to their history classes every day. But that doesn't mean they're free from the public and political pressure to teach Australia's past – far from it.

The media discussion surrounding the Australian History Summit in August 2006 reminded me what Margaret from

Hobart had said earlier that year about teaching the nation's past. When I asked her how she reconciled those public expectations about kids' national knowledge, she sighed and gave a look of exasperation. Knowing Australian history was necessary, Margaret agreed, but the political pressure to teach Australia's story was frustrating: 'Oh look, you read in the paper all the time about the history the kids should know and I keep thinking, "Right, come into a classroom and teach it". It doesn't work.'[17]

Margaret wasn't the only teacher who struggled with the competing civic emphases on national knowledge on the one hand and student interest and engagement on the other. At an independent school in Darwin, Annabel also felt Australian history 'should be a compulsory component of a broader history subject'. But it shouldn't be too parochial, she added: 'I think only teaching Australian history would be boring and very narrow minded as well. I think there's a danger of ramming Australian history down kids' throats.' Jessica, a teacher in Brisbane, was similarly uncertain when asked if she thought Australian history should be mandated in school. 'Yes. Yes I do,' she said. 'What elements are compulsory then is a much more problematic issue. I wouldn't like to go to a situation where we have a lengthy checklist that has to be signed off on.'[18]

It's a lesson that some politicians have had to learn the hard way. At the summit, former New South Wales Premier Bob Carr remembered how responses from teachers forced him to change the thrust of a mandatory Australian history syllabus developed under his government. In 1997 the New South Wales Board of Studies formally decreed one hundred hours of Australian history and civics in years 9–10, which would be concluded with a public examination. History teachers had initially been enthusiastic about the prospect of a mandatory syllabus – they thought any effort to cement the place of history in schools was to be celebrated. But once it was implemented, teachers felt the syllabus was overloaded with content and lacked broad interest and appeal for students.

Carr originally maintained that the mandatory Australian history course had been developed because it was imperative to teach core national knowledge.[19] Yet teachers quickly lost confidence. Post-compulsory history enrolments were declining as a result of the subject, and in a submission to the History Teachers' Association one teacher said that year 10 students 'are finding this course boring and deadly dull!'[20] Speaking on behalf of the association, Kate Cameron argued that 'a lot of damage' had been done because of the mandatory syllabus. 'Most teachers hate it because it is impossible to teach well,' she said.[21]

Students dutifully confirmed their teachers' growing concerns with underwhelming results in the compulsory exam. Of the 79 000 students who did the test in 2002, only 12 per cent received a result in band five or band six – the two highest brackets of achievement. (By contrast, about 25 per cent of students achieved this result in both science and maths, and about 30 per cent in English.) Many teachers felt the problem was the prescription of content. 'There is simply no time' to teach the course properly, one teacher complained, and this was 'leading to boring teaching and bored students'.[22]

Carr reflected on his mandatory course at the history summit, and insisted that while the subject should be compulsory in all schools, he wouldn't hold up the New South Wales experience 'as an unqualified ideal because it is clear it wasn't taught in an interesting way'. When Carr visited history classes in his state after the syllabus was first implemented, the response from teachers was pretty unequivocal. They thought the course was a burden and too content-heavy, he recollected. Meanwhile, added Carr, the students simply weren't interested:

'When I went to year 9 and 10 history classes and I said, "How many of you will be doing history for the HSC [Higher School Certificate]?", not too many hands went up.'[23]

After pleas from teachers and curriculum developers, the New South Wales syllabus was eventually rewritten more in line with their demands. Content was reduced so that students would be able to have more studies in depth, and the scope of the exam was reduced. But even now after the rewrite, not all New South Wales teachers are convinced. Michael, a history teacher from the state's south, agreed that Australian history ought to be mandatory, but felt that the balance still hadn't quite been reached. *Do you think that Australian history should be a compulsory school subject?*, I asked him. 'Yes, I think it should,' he agreed, 'but I think there's too much of it, and I think there's too little time for it. So I don't think this is a very good course.'[24]

The New South Wales experience is fresh in many teachers' minds around the country, and a few of them even warned me that any national attempt to follow their mandatory model could generate a negative reaction from both them and their students. Greg, who teaches at a girls' school in Brisbane, was categorical. 'Do I think it needs to be a compulsory subject as in New South Wales? Absolutely not! The reason being, if you put the words "compulsion" and "teenager" in the same sentence, it's a disaster, and you will get a backlash.' Jessica said she wasn't sure 'that anybody is enamoured with following the New South Wales model' in Queensland. 'To have mandatory things that have to be learned, and obviously taught and then tested, builds resentment that I'm sure is very counterproductive.'[25]

The Queensland Studies Authority, responsible for curriculum development in that state, also expressed concern about any mandated approach which was 'stipulating, you know, at this point they do this, this and this'. Leanne Iselin, the Principal Education Officer in Standards and Assessment at the authority, explained the fine line between cementing history's importance in the curriculum and turning kids off it: 'What I'm concerned about is that by having a set amount of time at every year level, you actually switch kids off. And you could end up with the reverse – that kids hate history. They're *there*, but they're not loving it.'[26]

Teachers elsewhere around the country expressed similar concern about crowding the subject with too much content. The day after the summit I spoke with Neil, a Canberra history teacher, who agreed with the effort to make Australian history a compulsory component of any school curriculum, 'but if it's compulsory it has to be well done,' he qualified. 'There's been a lot of talk about a "renaissance" in Australian history by making it compulsory. But if we don't get it right it will be a funeral wake.'[27]

Teachers like Neil, Jessica and Greg aren't troublemakers. They're not trying to stonewall a national curriculum intervention out of obstinacy. They're passionate and committed history teachers who simply want their experiences in the classroom and in curriculum development to be at least acknowledged in the public discussion over teaching the past. Those key 'facts and dates' that look so obvious in a media release or newspaper column aren't quite so easy to convey on a Friday afternoon in a class full of noisy, tired teenagers.

Students aren't immune to this tension between the pressures for national knowledge and generating interest and engagement in class. Like their teachers, they essentially agreed that Australian history was important to know – but then there was the question of how to teach it. In Melbourne, these year 12 students debated the prospect of mandatory Australian history with each other:

> *Do you think Australian history should be compulsory?*
>
> **Chris:** *No.*
>
> **Kaleb:** *Yes.*
>
> **Chris:** *I guess I'm not a maths person, so maths people won't be humanities people. It should [be compulsory] in the earlier years, like you need to sort of know where you're coming from, but in later years, people aren't gunna like it or enjoy it, and they won't do well.*
>
> **Kaleb:** *To me, history is very relevant to how we live our lives. We learn from our mistakes and if we learn we won't make those mistakes again – well unfortunately we are, but I personally attribute some of the current affairs to people's lack of knowledge of what has happened in the past.*[28]

Both students sense the importance of learning Australian history – as Chris says, 'you need to sort of know where you're coming from'. But they're just as aware that being forced to learn the subject risks turning them off it. It's a delicate balance all right: how do we teach that knowledge *and* make sure it really engages students?

A group from a public school on the New South Wales Central Coast who debated the merits of compulsory Australian history were similarly torn. Jill, from year 9, said she thought the subject was necessary to study: 'I do. I can't understand why other states don't learn about it, because it's really important that we do.' Les, a year 10 student, agreed that Australian history was important, but he wasn't sure that mandating the subject was the best way to go about it: 'I don't think it should be compulsory, because I've always found from personal experience that if you try and make things compulsory it's the fastest way to make people *not* interested.'[29]

Meanwhile, a group of year 12 students in Perth tossed the same question about in their interview. Garry was adamant that Australian history shouldn't be compulsory. His classmate Eva tended to agree. 'I can't say I'd look forward to doing it,' she admitted. But for Maddison, the subject was essential knowledge, 'because you need to *know* it,' he said. 'I'm not sure that you need to know it in the same depth as we do in history class, but you need the knowledge, the basic knowledge of it.'[30]

A lot of students are certainly convinced Australian history is too important to leave to choice alone. But, like their teachers, many of them are also worried that mandating the subject may be the quickest way to turn their schoolmates off it. I guess I stand with Neil from Canberra on this one: Australian history is critically important to know and understand, but if it's going to be mandated 'it has to be done well'.

The whole question about compulsory Australian history is such a problematic proposition that a few of the teachers I spoke with gave completely different responses in the same breath: on the one hand it's vital to know about, they insisted; but on the other, any effort to shovel it into kids could have the opposite effect. Gail teaches at a small rural school in Tasmania, and said that 'there are some things that are essential for people to think, know and understand, and I have a very firm belief that there are some aspects of our history that's important for us to have an understanding of, in terms of who we are and where we've come from'. Then she qualified herself: 'But I don't think people should be forced to teach anything they don't want to. And if it's compulsory does it mean it's going to be a better quality of teaching of history? Will it make you do history more? Make you enjoy the subject? I don't know.'[31]

For Margaret in Hobart, the issue was just as complicated. 'There are basics about geography and history that kids need to understand who they are, and so yeah, I feel we need some guidelines drifted in somewhere,' she said. 'But I never want to see a situation that says you'll teach this to this person on this day and in this way, because you have to come from where kids are at.'[32]

Teachers found this question about compulsory Australian history hardest to answer. It's politically loaded, for a start. In a year when the subject hit the headlines following their prime minister's call for a renewal of history education, and again, when their federal minister arranged a summit to push for a national history curriculum, a number of teachers felt I was putting them on the spot.

Greg grinned when I asked him about mandating the subject – 'this is a trick question,' he said. 'That's a really hard question,' replied Daniel, another Queensland teacher. Over in Perth, when I asked the retired history teacher Jan Bishop whether Australian history should be compulsory, she also hesitated for a second: 'Oh, that's a difficult one,' she answered. 'I would say history should be a compulsory subject for a couple of years but not compulsory throughout the whole of K–12.' But it's not as simple as just mandating the subject, she added: 'History is important but my feeling is, whenever history is made compulsory there's been a turning off of students and teachers because of being under compulsion to teach certain topics.'[33]

At the Department of Education and Community Services in South Australia, Terry Woolley similarly questioned what I was trying to elicit in the interview: 'when you ask should Australian history be compulsory, the answer is yes, but just whose history are we talking about?' he wondered. 'Is it John Howard's view of history? Is it my view of history? Is it your own? And who decides that? So straight away you are into the question of what history is being taught.'[34]

Is compulsory Australian history the answer to poor student knowledge and interest in the subject? Teachers agreed it's vital to teach, but there was certainly no consensus on how to make it work. Sandra, a history teacher from Perth, says students 'want to learn but if they just had it quite ad hoc and if it's taught badly, you know, it really impedes their willingness to learn it again'. Echoing her views, Brian, who teaches at a public school on the New South Wales Central Coast, was also cautious about how to mandate the subject. 'Whenever you make it compulsory, you destroy a lot of the interest,' he commented. 'So ultimately, I guess, I think it's probably important, but I think you need creative programming, and a genuine commitment to engage students, not to teach them facts.'[35]

So the issue isn't so much whether or not Australian history is important, but whether a really good course can be developed, with a dedicated bunch of teachers who have access to adequate professional development and resources. You can laugh at me here – sure, it's the same old, same old; teachers and students have lived through countless curriculum developments and teaching strategies to make Australian history 'more interesting' and 'relevant' – but when was the last time their views actually *directed* public debate over a national history curriculum? Unless these classroom perspectives play a real and distinct role in developing a national history curriculum (this is where it's going to have to be implemented, after all), it's doubtful whether any effort to mandate the subject will be 'doable', 'teachable' or 'sustainable'.

How can we get a national curriculum right?

By the time they finish school, students will almost certainly have studied *some* topics on Australian history, such as pre-contact Indigenous history, colonisation, convicts, the goldrushes, colonial self-government, federation, World War I, the conscription debate, the Depression, World War II, immigration, women's rights, the Vietnam War, Indigenous rights, and contemporary political history. These topics provide the content for Australian history in curriculum documents around the country and, taken together, they form a relatively coherent narrative of Australia's past.

The problem is that while a few students will study all of them, most will only learn bits and pieces here and there, with the possible exception of New South Wales. The topics are rarely taught sequentially: some students may have studied nothing about convicts or Australia's political history, while others complain they study federation year after year. We don't know what students have learnt because there's no nation-wide prescription for teaching Australian history. So is a mandatory national approach to Australian history the answer?

The response to this question was mixed. Like some of the comments from Queensland teachers and curriculum designers, the Curriculum Council in Western Australia were also cautious of an Australian history curriculum developed centrally from Canberra. Kerry Boyd, one of the curriculum officers at the council, said that students in more isolated areas deserved a history course that's as relevant to them as any class in the eastern states. 'For some of our country towns that are so far away, talking about Sydney or Botany Bay is just alien to them,' she explained.

That reality is pretty different from my experience growing up in Sydney, where our high school organised an annual year 10 history and civics camp to Canberra. We visited Parliament House, the High Court and the Electoral Commission. Looking back, I don't remember feeling *particularly fortunate* to receive the information sheets we had to fill out during the trip: Who is Australia's foreign minister? What is the difference between the House of Representatives and the Senate? And so on.

But for a number of the schools I visited this sort of trip would simply be an expensive luxury. Despite financial assistance from the federally funded Parliament and Civics Education Rebate, many schools still don't have the means to visit the capital. 'A lot of our schools don't even go to Perth on excursion, let alone Canberra,' says Kerry Boyd. 'If you're in Kalgoorlie you go to Esperance, if you're in Meekatharra you go off to Broome, places like that. So yes, Parliament House isn't somewhere they're likely to go.'[36]

Julie Fisher, the Principal Education Officer for SOSE at the Tasmanian Department of Education, also talked about this curricular challenge of maintaining local perspectives within any national history. Australian history is important 'for all students', she agreed, 'but I wouldn't like to see a mandated compulsory curriculum that says each grade studies particular things. I think that we still should be leaving that up to school communities to decide what's relevant and meaningful for their students, and also we need to allow for the curriculum to be differentiated to cater for all learners.'[37]

I'm the first to admit my own bias towards having some sort of nationally co-ordinated curriculum. I love Australian history, I have that slight missionary zeal when it comes to teaching it, and I often felt a personal twinge of disappointment when any of the kids said they hated it in their interviews. But Boyd and Fisher have a point: students need to connect to the story they're being taught. It's no use *solely* focusing on the First Fleet at school in Perth if Western Australia's convict history can help demonstrate the same ideas.

This national question certainly isn't new for those who've worked federally. Tony Brian-Davis said it was a constant issue when he was managing the Commonwealth History Project. There was an ongoing tension between the local and regional perspectives of schools and the national perspective of the federal government: at one end, he said, the government has a 'national picture of what they think should be done ... And at the other end you've got the classroom teacher whose job is to try and make it work.' While the aim is certainly there to produce more nuanced, sympathetic accounts of the nation's history, 'that may or may not be with suitable resources', Brian-Davis admitted. 'It may be with an understanding that whoever said in Canberra, "this is how it should be done", has got no idea how it's going to fit in Adelaide or Dubbo or wherever.'[38]

The huge disparity between classrooms has been confirmed by my sojourns at various schools around the country. You don't have to be a teacher with twenty years' experience to realise that individual schools are far from equivalent. For Justine, who teaches at a public school in central Australia, it's not even a question of what Australian history to teach, but whether it can be taught at all:

> *Do you think Australian history should be compulsory?*
>
> *No I don't, because I mean there are some students that it really isn't relevant to, and really it's much more important for them to be able to read and write and get the basic skills than it is for them to be trying to learn stuff that they really don't want to learn. But at the same time I think it should be available for those people who want it.*[39]

Compared with more privileged schools around the country, Justine's experience isn't typical by any means. But alongside schools in similarly remote or disadvantaged areas, what she has to deal with every day is hardly out of the ordinary. Getting kids to come to school is the priority here, let alone conveying the facts of Australia's history.

Justine's school is particularly confronting because it challenges the idea of a more co-ordinated and coherent national approach to history teaching. It certainly complicated my own belief in greater curriculum consistency. How would Justine's class be accommodated in a national history curriculum, for instance? And how can we tell her that teaching Australian history is as critical as boosting attendance or basic literacy?

Yet, how else are we going to tackle the repetitive nature of so much Australian history teaching if the curriculum isn't co-ordinated somehow? And unless some effort is made to define the national story, students' knowledge of the past will continue to remain patchy and unformed. The desire for a more coherent national approach to history teaching rubs uneasily against the specific curriculum needs of individual schools.

When I spoke with Deborah at her public senior college in Canberra, she insisted that teachers shouldn't be forced to teach a narrowly prescriptive representation of Australian history. But she was still worried about the way her students seem to have disengaged from the subject. They say things like, 'I've done that, don't want to do it any more,' Deborah lamented, yet these students 'need to know their modern Australian history. They need to know about the Dismissal and about Chifley, and they just don't *know* these things.' At a selective public school in Sydney, Therese said she was really conscious of the effect in the classroom since Australian history had been mandated in New South Wales. While she noticed that quite a few students who would never have picked the subject were now learning about the nation's past, the lessons weren't nearly so engaging as those with her elective classes, where students had chosen the subject themselves.[40]

Even students sense the tension between needing to 'know these things' and actually generating some class interest. Tahlia, a year 12 student from a public school in outer Melbourne, lamented the state of her patchy historical knowledge, although she wasn't exactly sure how she would engage with the material. 'I think something they should probably cover – it's not very interesting, but they should probably cover it – is the prime ministers. Because I wouldn't have a clue what was the first prime minister, or any of them. Menzies is like the only one, and Curtin, and Howard (of course!).'[41]

At another public school in central Australia, a group also debated the problem of mandating Australian history:

> **Edie:** *I'd really like to go more into politics and just really get into the background of politics and just how that's all gone. As I mentioned before, my little cousin is seven. She just moved to America last year and they hammer it into them and she knows all of the presidents, when they were running, how long they ran for, all of the first ladies' names, how many children they had – and she's seven! I don't think any of us could name five American presidents, let alone three Australian prime ministers. We're just not taught that stuff. We're just not offered that information.*
>
> **Rory:** *But if you really think about it, most of the kids in the class, if you did start teaching that stuff no one would listen at all.*
>
> **Anthony:** *Yeah, the students and stuff just aren't interested in learning it, and the people that wanna learn it get left out, because the teachers don't even go near because they know that they won't get a good response from the class.*[42]

These kids have a strong sense of the importance of learning Australian history content. There are certain things they want to know, and feel they *should* know. But they're also aware of how difficult it is to teach it. I got the sense that the students felt they were being held back by their school's circumstances. The curriculum is tailored to encourage Indigenous attendance and participation – and even Rory and Anthony understand that a more content-driven curriculum would alienate their Indigenous classmates even more from a school which has tried so hard to be inclusive.

The nature of curriculum development is always going to be a balancing act in that regard. The more particularly it caters for different areas, schools or even students, the less coherence it is able to ensure. And yet, individual schools and teachers *must* find aspects of that story to connect their students with – otherwise there'll be no historical engagement at all.

If it's that hard to accommodate all students at one school in central Australia, just think how difficult it will be on a national scale. Another history summit participant, Jenny Lawless (who's also the History Inspector at the New South Wales Board of Studies), explained in her interview the size of the task: 'I think with the summit working group it's going to be difficult trying to have a broad enough umbrella for states to do things in their way, and of course they've got distinct state interests as well to be taught,' she said. 'So it has to be broad enough to do that, and that's going to be a real challenge.'[43]

After the calls for a 'root and branch renewal' and for a history 'renaissance' in schools, we find ourselves in a position where the importance of Australian history has surely been confirmed but the challenge of making it interesting is still before us. Teachers I spoke with also sensed the importance of this cusp we seem to have reached. Amy works at an independent girls' school in Canberra, and without question agrees that 'Australian history has to be taught. There's no doubt in my mind about that,' she said; 'but,' she continued (and this is the big but), 'it shouldn't be in a vacuum. You can't *just* teach Australian history.'[44]

Neil, another Canberra history teacher, was just as adamant about the importance of developing a national curriculum, and just as cautious about how that should be undertaken. 'What we don't want is a grand narrative and what we don't want is a chronological, fact-driven syllabus,' he said. 'We want a syllabus, a curriculum, which opens kids up to the problems and the breadth of history. We don't want them following a single train track towards a predetermined end.'[45]

These teachers show that any curriculum response to the pressures to teach Australian history must not be at the expense of student engagement. There were considerable discrepancies among all teachers I spoke with over how mandated or how centrally composed any history curriculum should be. But all agreed about the importance of teaching the nation's past, and all hoped it would expand rather than reduce students' historical interest.

I'm also hopeful that developing a national curriculum doesn't have to be a mutually exclusive choice between interesting subject matter and learning 'the facts'. Teachers have to constantly juggle public pressures to teach 'our nation's' history with the particular demands of their classes and their students. That's why there's such uncertainty about whether a national curriculum will strengthen the subject or simply turn kids off it. After all the hoo-haa surrounding the history summit, it's pretty clear that there's general acceptance about the significance of the subject. But teachers, curriculum designers and students don't want Australian history to alienate the very people it's supposed to inspire.

CHAPTER 5

History in the classroom

> *How don't you like learning history?*
>
> **Trace:** *Out of a textbook.*
>
> **Cory:** *Copying straight out of a textbook.*
>
> **Trace:** *And not questioning it, just believing it.*
>
> **Cory:** *Just regurgitating information.*
>
> Year 11 students, public high school, Brisbane

What kids hate

We can probably all remember an awful history class we had: the teacher that just went on and on; the same boring handouts on explorers or convicts or gold; or the students who didn't want to be there and made it unbearable for everyone else. The cliché that history is deadly dull, and often taught by an archetypal relic from the past itself, is far removed from the sorts of classes I saw. But it still has popular currency. In *Harry Potter*, even Professor Binns (the History of Magic teacher) is so past it that he's become a ghost, droning on and on while his students dutifully try to copy down the names and dates of famous witches and magicians.[1] Sure, this is the light relief of fiction and fantasy, but the sentiment still rings true: history can come alive in the classroom, but just as surely it can also be ruined.

The gripes kids have today don't have quite the same delicious imagery as a history class in a Harry Potter novel, but they paint a readily identifiable picture of what makes the subject dull. I asked each student to describe the type of history class they didn't like, and most were pretty candid. Justin, a year 12 student in Perth, didn't enjoy just using textbooks, 'because reading about something's not really the same as talking about something'. Jiang in Brisbane didn't like just taking down notes: 'Especially analysis that somebody else does, and you just have to copy it down, because part of the analytical thing is actually coming up with it yourself and thinking through it or something,' she said. 'Whereas if you're copying it's just the words on the paper and you don't get to think about it like that, and you don't learn quite as well.'[2]

Most forms of rote learning came up as students' least appealing approach to the subject. At an independent school on the outskirts of Adelaide, Matilda hated learning 'Dates

– trying to remember all the dates'. And students frequently criticised teaching approaches that relied too heavily on the textbook at the expense of more interactive forms of learning. While they acknowledged there was a place for learning 'the facts', they felt an over-emphasis on content took the interest out of the subject. This was certainly true for Maddison, a year 12 student from Perth, who didn't like learning history when the lessons were 'Entirely textbook focused. I mean, textbooks are important for a lot of it, but entirely textbook – especially the textbooks we get – is horrible.' 'Yeah,' agreed his classmate Eva, 'I don't like the kind of style where you just read and answer questions. It's okay if you're reading and kind of talking about it.'[3]

When I spoke with a group of students at a public school in outer suburban Melbourne, Jamie said that she also found history was most boring when she was just 'Reading a textbook, when you have to like read three pages of a textbook, and then the teacher's like, "Do the questions", but you don't completely grasp the idea of what the textbook is actually telling you, because no one else talks about it'.[4] Jamie might have talked using the ungrammatical 'likes' of her cohort (and my own, I confess), but her *dislikes* were even clearer: relying on textbooks, just focusing on content, and the absence of any class discussion made for a boring history lesson. The comments of these year 11 students in Brisbane were also pretty typical of the focus group conversations I had around the country. Students felt the one sure way to kill a history class was an excessively content-driven and teacher-focused lesson without adequate conversation among the students themselves:

> *Are there ways you really don't like learning history?*
>
> Miranda: *Overheads!*

> **Chloe:** *Just having the teacher talk at you for the whole lesson, like stand up there and talk, while you sit.*
>
> **Linda:** *Yeah, you lose interest.*
>
> **Miranda:** *You just sit and listen and take down a couple of notes from an overhead or something.*
>
> **Chloe:** *You have to actually talk about history, and come to your own conclusions about it.*[5]

Such comments probably won't surprise educators who deal with school students every day, but I was quite taken by the seriousness and articulateness of their message. Students frequently expressed their frustrations with teaching methods that they felt hindered the subject rather than opened it up for further exploration. As Chloe says, you need to 'talk about history' in order to develop your own understandings.

Furthermore, while these students were perhaps characteristically opinionated about the things they *didn't* like, they also had ideas about tackling them. Again, I think their comments need to be taken seriously here because they seemed to take the question seriously in their interviews. Only one student gave a teasing answer about wanting history to be more of a bludge when he asked for 'Less homework, maybe' – and even then his quip should be read in the context of a bunch of boys trying to have a bit of a laugh at the end of their interview.[6]

When the group of Canberra year 11 students discussed whether they would change anything about the way they learnt history, Jade pleaded for change within the curriculum itself, demanding 'No more repetition!' Her response is pretty typical of students' views about topics like federation and Indigenous history, which they feel are endlessly revisited throughout their school years. For other students, the actual class needed to be approached differently. Erica, a year 11 student from Melbourne, said that 'The textbooks just kill ya. They're so draining.' Aiden, a year 9 student at the same school, hoped for 'a little bit more discussion. We could do that more.'[7]

In Tasmania, Allie said that she'd 'like to have more hands-on sort of stuff, so do activities and thinking in ways of other people and that sort of stuff, because most of the stuff that's read out or I read goes straight over my head. But if I'm watching something or actually *doing* something I find it easier to learn.' A number of students talked about the importance of using different learning activities and approaches to break up their lessons. At an Islamic college in western Sydney, Yasmin liked excursions 'because it motivates you practically. It's a different setting, different environment, and it's also really good to have discussions,' she said. 'I don't really like it when your teacher just says, "Alright, here's a page, you read it and you answer the questions". That's quite boring. I mean it's more practical to have discussion, I like the way they talk a lot – as long as they don't go off the track.'[8]

It's unfortunate that not every class can do the activities they want. Andie goes to a public girls' school in Sydney and described the limitations she and her classmates faced with history. 'I think it's hard with history,' she said. 'Like, I'd say more practical stuff, something we can interact with a bit more.' Andie's teacher also wished he was able to offer more to his students, but felt constrained by the time pressures in the New South Wales mandatory curriculum as well as the cost and logistics of organising history excursions: 'We would like to do more – just getting the kids out of school is always a complex thing, but it's of great value.'[9]

Students at a rural public school in southern New South Wales begged for more history fieldwork – a little melodramatically, to be sure, but their case was a valid one:

> *Would you change anything about the way history is taught at your school?*
>
> Leo: *Have an excursion.*
>
> Tristan: *At least one, please!*[10]

In New South Wales, where Australian history is mandatory in years 9 and 10, students are required to do a 'site study' (conduct history fieldwork) to complete the course. But a number of the teachers I spoke with felt so rushed covering the content that they weren't able to do all the activities they wanted, and felt that the excursions they did manage were sometimes cursory. Of course, I can't know how many teachers across the state have this same experience, but the fact that it was brought up by four out of five teachers I interviewed there reveals a degree of curriculum constraint and pressure, which some teachers clearly feel reduces the potential of the course itself.

This issue again raises important questions about how a mandatory history curriculum might be imposed nationally. Learning historical context, and therefore content, is an essential component of historical understanding. But at what point does only learning content start to limit actually *doing* history in the classroom? It's worrying if a worthy syllabus component like the site study is sidelined by teachers, who feel they need to race through the content of the course in time for the exam.

Beyond New South Wales, the main problem felt by teachers and students was access to educational resources more broadly – and this was especially true for public schools and schools in disadvantaged or remote areas. Teachers and students who wanted to use a variety of classroom approaches were invariably limited by what they could get their hands on. Even the keenest and most committed teachers, compared to many better-off schools, often had second-rate material to teach the same history. Students at a public senior college in Canberra were scathing about the quality of their history resources in class. 'They need to get some new resources,' said Lee. Gunita agreed: 'The videos are shocking, and some of the textbooks, too, are like from 1988, and that's how old *we* are.'[11]

Of course, some schools are more fortunate – and it is over this issue of access to resources that the differences between school sectors were most visible. While Lee and Gunita couldn't even get decent videos or textbooks at their Canberra public school, Amy, who heads the History Department at an independent girls' school nearby, was able to be much more hopeful in her answer:

> *Well, I have to say that my main instruction with all of my staff here is that it must be inspiring. If you don't catch their interest, then what's wrong with the way that you're teaching it? Now we have fabulous resources here. You can have everything – you name it, they can have it. They can ask me for it and I will budget for it, so there isn't any excuse at all for anything being presented in a boring fashion. It's just got to come alive, and it's got to be, I suppose it's the sort of thing that's made to live.*[12]

While there weren't discernible differences in the passion or commitment of history teachers between the government and non-government sectors, their resources were often poles apart. Some wealthier schools had interactive classrooms, where students could be online simultaneously with the teacher, they had up-to-date audiovisual equipment, and students had laptop computers.

However, teachers at many of the state schools I visited were frequently frustrated by their access to resources and support. For some of them, even scraping together enough money for an excursion was difficult. Either history wasn't supported as a subject in the schools or remoteness made excursions very difficult to organise. David wished he could be more original teaching history at his public school in central Australia:

> I tend to use textbooks but I don't think it's the best way. I think personal experience for the kids – you know, excursions and role-plays – I think that's the best way to do it. But we're a little bit resource restricted here, plus for us to go to any of the wartime sites for example, we have to travel to Darwin and that's two days, extremely expensive. It's a thousand kilometres each way.[13]

In Tasmania, Margaret was also bound by the financial situations of her students and her school. I asked whether they had many excursions to local historical sites: 'Not nearly as many as we want to do,' she replied. 'It's a constant hassle for the school. The funding is the main problem ... really, the main thing that has limited our excursions has been money. It is a constant battle. We talk the whole time about what we want to do and what we can't do.'[14]

This is where we start getting into some delicate political territory. Obviously, the disparity among schools is a vexed and ongoing educational concern: it's great for those students who have access to such fabulous resources, and it's awful that other classes feel so limited. To be honest, I often felt a *little pang* of envy on behalf of those classes when I visited some of the wealthier independent and Catholic schools. But I also don't want to make these financial differences between the schools seem so extreme that their history classes are no longer comparable.

There were vast gulfs between the experiences of students at the public high school in outer suburban Melbourne I visited and the independent girls' school in town. But there was also a chasm between that Melbourne public school and its counterparts in central Australia. My point is that despite these financial differences, most of which I would love to see overcome, the attitudes to Australian history and the way students and teachers engaged with the subject were relatively consistent among all the schools I visited; the way teachers and students described the dynamics of their classrooms, both good and bad, were repeated again and again across the country. And this means that good history teachers and good history classes weren't just confined to the schools with more money.

The 'history teacher'

Despite the various classroom limitations that teachers and students described, they were equally adamant about the key ingredient for a great history lesson: the teacher. Perhaps this is to be expected – I certainly remember taking subjects at school and university simply because I liked the teacher or, much like a mechanic or a dentist, a friend recommended them. Some students I knew at uni even became teacher 'groupies', taking every course they could with a beloved lecturer.

For the school students I spoke with, what they liked and didn't like in their history classes so often came down to this one factor. Jackie, a year 10 student from Perth, said: 'If you've got a good teacher that enjoys it it's much better for you because you can relate to them'. 'Yeah,' added her classmate Sophie, 'some teachers just don't.' Keira goes to a public high school near Darwin and admits that she's 'just not into history', but she did make this concession: 'I reckon like a really enthusiastic teacher would do it well. But if you get like a real boring teacher that everyone hates, no one's going to listen. If you get a really good teacher that everyone likes then everyone will want to listen.'[15]

At the other end of the country, students from a small public school in Tasmania's south-east also talked about the importance of the teacher for enjoying the subject. In an animated discussion about what makes a good history class, Aysha reckoned 'It depends what teacher you're getting.' Karen thought so too: 'Some teachers just dictate it to you and some teachers take you through it,' she said. 'The teacher's important. I mean if the teacher just stands there and mumbles half an encyclopaedia out to you, it's just going to go in one ear and out, and you're going to be half asleep on the table.'[16]

Teachers were often described in this binary way: bored teachers made for boring classes, but enthusiastic teachers could turn even the most recalcitrant students around. In Adelaide, Lydia thought that the attitude of the teacher was critical. 'I think it *really* depends on the teacher you have,' she said. 'One year I had a teacher I really didn't like and it was just hard to feel connected to the subject because it just seemed so irrelevant and so boring. If you have a good teacher it's a lot easier to be motivated and be interested in what the subject's about.' Andie, who goes to a public girls' school in Sydney, said she was fortunate because, 'We've got a teacher who really wants us to learn, but I've had teachers in the past who, they've either been teaching for too long or they're not passionate about it.'[17]

Morgan in Canberra also found the enthusiasm of her teacher infectious and wished all teachers could draw their students in like she did:

> *I also think that a teacher has to be able to make other students who don't think they're that interested in learning about history, um, I think they need to be able to have a classroom where everyone is interested. Like I think that would be a really difficult thing to do, but like our teacher is just a really good teacher and she's able to engage people who don't even think that they're interested in history.*[18]

A few history teachers I spoke with even mentioned the influence of a particular teacher on their own careers – teachers who had led them to choose history teaching. Cameron works at a Catholic boys' school in Perth, and I asked him whether he liked history teaching: 'I love it,' he insisted. That love had been ignited by his history teacher, and the connection Cameron had experienced was exactly what he tried to re-create with his students in turn. 'I guess I've always just had an interest in it and it was sparked by my own history teacher when I was at school,' he said. 'And I know that I've said this throughout the interview, I just really enjoy finding out why the world is the way it is and that's something that I really enjoy passing on to the students.'[19]

After such devastating assessments from students about how uninteresting they found Australian history, I have to admit that I found these descriptions of mutual admiration and respect in the history class slightly infectious. In Darwin, Tani said, smiling, 'all of the teachers that we've got here for history are like *soooo* ace, like they make the subject.' Her classmate Natalie thought so too: 'You can just see the passion that they hold for it as well, and that's something that's really great.' At the public girls' school in Sydney, students talked about the problems of some classes they had been in; 'But our teacher is really good,' Jasmine quickly added. 'I think his overall attitude is very encouraging too. When you do something right he gives you a lot of praise.' Chen thought so too: 'He's very positive.' (And I should probably add here that their teachers weren't present in these interviews.)[20]

For their part, history teachers also couldn't help but notice the importance of simple passion for getting their kids interested the subject. Ellen from Darwin says that she can't bear it when a child says in class, 'I hate history. It's so boring.' If 'anyone says that to me I go, "Oh shit, what's been done to this child?".' On the other hand, says Mary in Brisbane, 'you can make anything alive and interesting if you find it alive and interesting'. In Melbourne, Jean also thought the vital ingredient for a great class was personal interest. 'I think what you've got to have is passion,' she said. 'If you're interested in the subject you'll find a way of getting into it with the kids. So you find something that excites you and therefore then you transfer that excitement.'[21]

Lots of students were highly critical of their history education, but positive comments from the classroom like these also show how successful history teaching can form lasting and meaningful connections between teachers and students. That many of them had finally found the subject interesting was no doubt down to the fact that they were being taught by enthusiastic and experienced teachers who were devoted to the subject.

The classrooms I visited were hardly warm and fuzzy 'love-ins', yet the passion that teachers felt for history clearly influenced how their students responded. In their study of what makes an influential teacher, sociologists Andrew Metcalfe and Ann Game describe this engagement as a sort of 'pedagogic love' – the connection teachers have with their subject and their teaching that students see as inspiring and infectious.[22] Love is a strong word for teaching, but it came up again and again in the interviews with teachers, many of whom said they loved their job, and thought the key to any success as a history teacher was a love of the subject.

While a number of teachers talked about being a passionate teacher more generally, others talked specifically about the critical importance of being trained in history in order to teach the subject well. I read their repeated insistence on the importance of qualified history teachers as a professional response to those students who complain of boring classes with narrow historical and educational approaches: in other words, if there were more trained history teachers, history classes would be significantly improved.

Sally teaches at a public high school in regional Victoria, and strongly advocated proper history training for history teachers. 'Well if I had my way, the main thing is that we'd have trained history teachers teaching history,' she said. 'I think our courses are really good but what we're lacking is trained history teachers and I think that's a real concern.' Cameron in Perth also stressed the importance of expertise in history for those teaching the subject. 'I think that the teachers that teach history also need to know their subject and they also need to know how to teach it,' he insisted. 'You can't just get someone who is an English teacher or someone who's from another subject area and get them in to teach history because unless they're specifically trained in how to teach it well then it's not going to be enjoyed by the students.'[23]

Their professional concern about the lack of teacher training for history is nothing new. In 2000, Tony Taylor published his National Inquiry into the state of history education, and the issue of qualified history teachers was already raising significant concern. Another study conducted by the Australian Education Union in 2000 found that 57.9 per cent of schools had teachers teaching outside their area of curriculum expertise. And in rural districts this figure was as high as 77.1 per cent. History teachers were quick to respond to those worrying statistics. Jacqualine Hollingworth, who was the Education Officer of the History Teachers' Association of Victoria at the time, said in a newspaper report about the study that she frequently had teachers who had never taught history ringing up to ask the difference between a primary and secondary source.[24]

Such anxiety is still pronounced, as these interviews reveal. Marco teaches history at a public school in the outer suburbs of Melbourne and was especially concerned about the way the subject was organised in his state. 'I think a lot of people haven't been trained in history and that has really been causing a lot of damage,' he said.[25] He thought the issue of teacher training had been exacerbated by the curriculum decision to combine history with other subjects such as geography and economics into the interdisciplinary Studies of Society and Environment (SOSE).

Marco himself had taught SOSE, he said, but didn't really feel qualified in the areas outside his own expertise that he was supposed to teach in – and if he felt like that, what use was it having teachers with no history background teaching Australian history? 'I'm not trained as a geography teacher and that makes it very difficult because I don't know how to teach the geography very creatively and I think that's a really big problem and that's seeped into schools,' he said. *Would you change anything about how history is taught at your school?* I asked. 'Oh yeah,' he continued. 'For a start I'd change the SOSE component and I'd bring back your electives like we used to have like fifteen years ago [where] year 10 kids would do a history elective or they'd do a geography elective and they'd have a qualified teacher doing that discipline and I think that made all the difference.'[26]

When I spoke with Marco, the Victorian Curriculum and Assessment Authority had recently returned to a discipline approach for teaching history, geography and economics in that state – although it still remains to be seen how that curriculum change will affect history teaching and teacher training in Victoria. In Queensland, too, teachers can now choose to teach history either as a discrete subject or via SOSE. Despite the curriculum shift in these states, however, SOSE is currently the primary mode for high school history teaching in Tasmania, South Australia, the Australian Capital Territory, the Northern Territory and Western Australia. And in those states and territories, a number of teachers reacted fiercely against the provision of *any* history within a SOSE program in their interviews.

Deborah from Canberra was particularly critical, and felt that SOSE had exacerbated kids' resistance to Australian history: 'In the ACT, and in other states presumably, it's sort of this mish-mash of SOSE, you know, Society and Environment. I've *always* thought that was horrible,' she said. This meant that 'what you're having is teachers who aren't trained – they're SOSE teachers, but they're not particularly history teachers, they're not trained in methodology, they might be legal studies teachers – and they've got to teach history. And I think something's going wrong. Kids are getting here and they do not want anything to do with Australian history. And that's a real shame.'[27]

If part of the problem lies with the lack of history teacher training, then part of any solution has to come from the university education faculties around Australia. It's true that many history teachers have studied history at university, have majored in the subject or have even completed honours or postgraduate degrees in history. But for some primary teachers, training in history method comprises as little as one third of a semester-long course on the subject during their four-year degree. As for secondary teachers, in many cases studying just one unit of history method is deemed sufficient. And that's not even taking into consideration those teachers who are forced to teach the subject due to school curriculum or timetable pressures but have no training in history method at all.

A number of teachers I spoke with explained the need for greater training in history method. Neil from Canberra was especially concerned: 'Teacher education at universities also obviously needs some attention, in that there are many people who come out of B.Eds [Bachelor of Education degrees], in particular for the primary, who have very limited experience of history as a methodology.' What's more, he continued, 'there are also a lot of graduates coming out of institutions with SOSE qualifications, but have limited exposure to history methodology'.[28]

I didn't mention the issue of SOSE in the interviews with students, so I was surprised when they often did of their own accord. (Because of this, it should be noted, there may have been other students who enjoyed this amalgamated approach to history but their views aren't represented here because they weren't specifically asked to comment.) When I asked a group of students in south-eastern Tasmania whether there was anything they would change about the way history is taught at their school, they mentioned the problem of SOSE. 'Well it's not really taught at our school,' said Hayley. 'Like, we don't have a history class,' Karen explained. Hayley continued: 'I think it should be a separate optional subject. Like, have it compulsory in grade 7 and 8, and then have it at 9 and 10 as an optional.'[29]

Students from an independent girls' school in Brisbane were also unconvinced by history's place in the curriculum, even though their own teacher supported SOSE. Jiang said she had 'really enjoyed the past couple of years' of senior history. She hadn't liked it so much up till now because 'once you get involved with like SOSE and things it really detracts from the historical things and it gets really boring sometimes because sometimes you get plonked in front of your book and it's like, "Read this, answer these questions, you're meant to know this by now", and it just gets really tedious after a while.' Her schoolmate Lily was also critical of the integrated approach: 'Going from grade 9 to 10,' she said, 'I definitely prefer doing just history, rather than the whole everything mushed together in SOSE.'[30]

Curriculum officials weren't afraid to voice their opinions on the SOSE debate either. Jenny Lawless from the New South Wales Board of Studies was adamant about the particularities of history education. She talked about 'the problem of SOSE-trained teachers who aren't trained historically or in historical method'. Lawless was trained as a 'geography teacher as well as history,' she said, and 'there are distinct geography skills that I would teach. But for me, there are distinct approaches and skills that lose out when the subjects and training are amalgamated, and I think that's a problem.'[31]

SOSE was definitely the most divisive and controversial issue among the teachers and curriculum designers I spoke with. All agreed on the need for trained history teachers, but a number of teachers insisted that history *could* be effectively taught within amalgamated subjects like SOSE. Some were even quite protective of the interdisciplinary approach. They believed it better catered for a range of different learners, rather than simply those who are more academically inclined, and they believed in its capacity to deal with broad-ranging issues such as ethics, human rights or democracy.

In Adelaide, Lara felt SOSE had expanded the potential of history rather than constrained it. 'I actually think that's great, you know, a lot of universities have broken down that discrete disciplinary stuff as well, and I think you can do much more exciting stuff by doing that,' she said. 'I think we're still doing it and we are making it much more interesting by combining it with legal studies and economics, and ultimately history's always been about those things anyway.' Despite assertions from his students that they preferred learning history on its own, Greg from Brisbane was also confident that Australian history could be taught effectively through SOSE. 'Inside the SOSE syllabus, there are compulsory Australian components, many of them,' he explained. 'You simply can't teach SOSE in

Queensland without doing some Australian history. It lives in the core learning outcomes of the syllabus.'[32]

In those states and territories where SOSE had been the primary approach used to teach history, curriculum designers were also keen to emphasise its strengths (even when some teachers expressed their resistance to SOSE). John McIntyre from the Department of Education and Training felt that the interdisciplinary approach worked well in the Australian Capital Territory: 'I don't think a stand-alone subject called "history" should be compulsory, but I think that learning in history should be compulsory,' he said. 'I think the debates around whether history should be a stand-alone subject or not are quite false debates. I'm not so much interested in how the learning is organised but that it happens in meaningful ways for students. And it can happen in a whole lot of different ways.'[33]

Questions about whether history should be taught as a discrete discipline or taught as part of an amalgamated approach have taken up a lot of space in Australian education circles over the past thirty or forty years. Debates over social studies in the 1960s and 70s merged into debates over SOSE after its inclusion in the 1989 Hobart Declaration on schooling, which was signed by all Australian education ministers and was in turn consolidated in the 1999 Adelaide Declaration. SOSE is one of the eight key learning areas agreed on in the Hobart Declaration, and within that history is primarily taught through the strand of 'Time, Continuity and Change'.

Importantly, though, not everyone adopted that curriculum model. Despite the national rhetoric of the Hobart Declaration, the New South Wales Government refused to sign on. While the rest of the country adopted SOSE in the compulsory years of schooling (history was retained in years 11–12), New South Wales held onto its discipline approach in high school. And because non-government schools aren't bound like state schools to state curricula, many of them also retained the discipline approach to history in their learning programs.

In other words, two parallel approaches to history education have continued to coexist in Australian high schools, which explains the serious divisions among teachers and curriculum designers. But it seems all this may soon change. Recent political and public concern over the state of history education has forced a return to the discipline approach by state and territory governments. The 2006 Australian History Summit confirmed the federal Coalition Government's intent to produce a national, discipline-based curriculum. While in opposition, the federal Labor Party also announced plans for a national curriculum that includes Australian history. Not to be outdone by their federal counterparts, however, in early 2007 the eight Labor premiers and chief ministers committed to returning the states and territories to a discipline approach on their own terms.[34]

It's not certain what this federal shift towards a national approach to history education will mean for the existing curriculum documents. Curriculum authorities in a number of states that I visited (Queensland and Tasmania, in particular) expressed a real reluctance to retreat from SOSE to what they felt was a more traditional, and more exclusive, approach to history education. There are also instances of very strong history programs within SOSE at many schools around the country. Yet it's clear from these interviews and from research into the status of history in schools that the interdisciplinary structure of SOSE has legitimated, and even institutionalised, the practice of non-history teachers heading history classes. And in turn, such practices have only increased discussion about the specificity of the history teacher and their role in the classroom. No doubt this debate will continue to rage in Australia for a few years yet – it'll take at least that long for any new curriculum documents to be drafted for a start. In the meantime, the place of the teacher in all this will continue to be at the centre of this history debate: namely, what makes a good history class, and how?

How do we teach it?

Students certainly weren't afraid to talk about the negative experiences they've had in their history classes. Teachers, too, spoke with considerable awareness and concern about the need for passionate, qualified educators in the subject. But that still leaves one more problem to ponder: how should history be taught?

This was the one question that every respondent answered in their interviews. Curriculum designers discussed how history should be taught in relation to curriculum development. Teachers described their most successful history classes. And in their focus groups, students each gave their views on how they learnt history best. To get the discussion rolling, I included a little list of teaching approaches for them to consider: for example, did they prefer excursions, classroom discussion/debates, guest speakers, textbooks, research projects or drama?

I had thought there'd be significant differences between the responses from teachers, but some of them gave me such a look of absolute incredulity before answering that I soon realised my assumption was way off the mark – of course they used *all* those things in their history classes! How else could it be taught? Gail from Tasmania said she used 'All of the above. Every part of the pedagogical repertoire.' In Melbourne, Jean said she couldn't imagine doing anything else: 'I don't think that there's only one way to teach history.'[35]

Far from having a single, favoured method, these experienced teachers talked about the importance of mixing up their approaches in class. For John, who teaches at a public girls' school in Sydney, the best classes use 'a variation of the text, the documentaries, the sources and the discussion'. 'I suppose it might appear cut and dry,' he said, 'but surprisingly enough, the kids come away with having a deep interest in these things. It grows on them – and they must go away and do a lot of researching and reading for themselves.' Deborah in Canberra also thought 'variety' was the key to a good history class: 'I think a variety of things, a combination of things – there's no one type in particular that works,' she said. 'And I think a good teacher will tailor their approach to the class that's sitting in front of them. It depends on the time of the year even, or what's coming up next, or their interest levels or the time of day that the lesson is on at. It's just sort of having different approaches at your finger-tips and being able to be confident enough to use them when you feel that the situation requires it.'[36]

So mixing up teaching wasn't just about taking different approaches into the classroom, but being able to utilise them in different ways within the same class even. In Adelaide, Stephen said that 'you need a whole suite of activities' to be a good teacher and respond to the needs of different classes as they arose. Neil, another Canberra teacher, also thought history teachers needed to be able to react to the flow of a particular class. 'Good teaching is a creative, an imaginative and a responsive activity in that it responds to student interest,' he said.[37]

For these teachers, history isn't something their students simply learn in class – it's something they do. And their confidence describing their different methods and approaches to the subject shows just how critical it is to have well-trained history teachers taking history classes.

We already know from students that their interest in the subject doesn't come from memorising 'what happened'. Teachers, too, thought the essence of successful history teaching came from passing on the skills of historical inquiry and analysis alongside the actual history itself. Brian, who teaches on the New South Wales Central Coast, finds history 'a really liberating, empowering subject to teach and students I believe walk out of my classrooms feeling more empowered than they do out of other subjects.'[38] For Jessica in Brisbane, conveying the complexity of the subject was also part of the challenge of teaching it:

> *I think within the framework of 'history is about inquiry' there are many strategies that work well and successfully, and teachers are different, and so styles are going to differ inevitably, and I guess that's the challenge of teaching – to find the mode of delivery that students are most receptive to in any context. So all of those things have a place. I don't know that there's a dominant, individual teaching approach.*[39]

It wasn't just teachers who took this attitude into the classroom. Curriculum designers were also keen to emphasise the importance of using a range of teaching approaches to cover the range of necessary content and skills – and they specifically designed their curriculum documents with that in mind. John Gore, the then Chief Education Officer for Human Society in Its Environment at the Department of Education and Training in New South Wales, insisted that 'Good teaching uses a range of strategies and resources. It is not desirable to prescribe pedagogy in the curriculum document (especially if they are mandatory as in New South Wales) without taking initiative away from the creative teacher.' In Victoria, John Firth, the Chief Executive Officer of the Victorian Curriculum and Assessment Authority, was similarly insistent on the importance of applying a plurality of pedagogical approaches in class: 'Well of course all of those things are appropriate,' he said. 'I'd turn it around and say if you relied on any one of those things exclusively it would be a pretty narrow approach.'[40]

This belief in the complexity of history may not drive debates in the media over what particular 'facts' this particular generation of students do or don't know, but it continues to guide the bulk of research on history education. Peter Lee heads the History Education Unit at the University of London and has written extensively on the depth of historical understanding that we should aim for in schools: 'Students need to know about the past or the whole exercise becomes pointless,' he admits. 'But understanding the discipline allows more serious engagement with the substantive history that students study, and enables them to *do* things with their historical knowledge.'[41]

Scholars such as Canada's Peter Seixas or Sam Wineburg in the United States tell the same story: 'historical understanding' means the capacity to critically engage with complex and often competing historical interpretations, and to reconcile the values of the past with those in the present – as well as developing knowledge of historical content. In Australia, the term 'historical literacy' has been used by history educationists Tony Taylor and Carmel Young to describe this rich taxonomy of historical skills.[42]

Given the growing understanding of the dimensions and importance of historical literacy in Australia and abroad, it's not surprising that curriculum officials strongly emphasised the complexities of historical understanding in their interviews. In New South Wales, Jenny Lawless from the Board of Studies described the range of skills required to learn history: 'our syllabuses are divided up into not only content, but also what we are trying to *do* with that is much more explicit. It's not just rote learning facts, which is a very lower order skill, but being able to actually engage in history.' In Victoria, Pat Hincks, the Curriculum Manager for Humanities at the Victorian Curriculum and Assessment Authority, explained the process as training students not to just learn about the past but to become historians themselves – and have the capacity to deal with different historical interpretations and historical sources. 'They develop skills in research and critical inquiry,' she said, 'so there is much emphasis on modelling the work of professional historians.'[43]

These approaches to historical understanding or historical literacy have also been taken into the classroom by many teachers, eager to convey the intricacies of the subject to their students (many of whom, as we know, have just about switched off). Mary teaches at a public school in Brisbane and says the reward for that approach is when her history classes really come alive: 'It's fun, it's good – you create critical kids,' she explained. 'The really bright ones will actually learn to challenge you as well as the texts and the sources and stuff'.[44]

Daniel, who teaches at a Catholic boys' school in Brisbane, said he also wanted to convey the full meaning of history: 'When the students are evaluating their sources, I remind them that I am one of their sources, and they need to make an evaluation of me too, and I'll talk openly about where my politics lie and my political philosophy.' At another Catholic boys' school in Adelaide, Stephen was similarly open about the skills of critical analysis he hoped to instil in his students: 'I like students to think, I like them to be critical thinkers. I like them to question what they're being fed, and even question what I might say to them as well.'[45]

I suppose it's par for the course that the views of these experienced teachers and curriculum designers reflect current academic thinking about history education. Yet students were also adamant that that's how they like to learn history. They might not have used terms like 'historical literacy' to describe the ways they best learnt the subject, but their engagement with history was strikingly similar to that of their teachers. When I asked a group of year 12 students from a public school in Darwin how they learnt history best, they said it was the questions raised in class by their active and encouraging teacher:

> Natalie: *We did a lot of debating last year, like arguing our different sides, and I think one of the really big components is having good teachers. I think what made that so interesting was that we had really good teachers who know their stuff and have like actively engaged us and they've questioned our opinions, and it's just been a really good experience.*
>
> Gabby: *I think on the whole, I don't want to speak for everyone in our history class, but I get the feeling that we all learn better through the discussions.*
>
> All: *Yeah.*
>
> Gabby: *Through being able to ask those questions and that sort of thing, rather than just reading dates out of a textbook. Although that is helpful in some instances, I think as a whole a lot of our learning has been through discussion.*[46]

These year 11 students at a public high school in Brisbane were also enthusiastic about learning in a critical classroom, where they could hear different perspectives and come to their own conclusions:

> *How do you think you learn history best?*
>
> Trace: *I dunno, I think when our teacher just stands in front of the classroom.*
>
> Cory: *Yeah, class discussion.*
>
> Trace: *She just gets really into it.*
>
> Kai: *She gets us to question the history, not just believe everything we're told.*
>
> Jenn: *And when she has the powerpoint going you get to hear people who have a different opinion to understand it better, because you have different people's views on it.*

> **Trace:** *We had a discussion thing for our assignment last term, and we got to hear what everyone had to say about everything.*[47]

In group after group, students described how comparing different perspectives through a mixture of class discussion, excursions and research projects made the subject more engaging. There were only a handful of exceptions from students who said they hated any sort of open-ended learning altogether and felt happiest in their history class when they could just read their textbooks. Roger, a year 10 student from Hobart said rote learning was his favourite: 'I learn better from reading from textbooks and stuff, like just finding out the facts and sitting in front of it I can relate to it easier than just going out and having to do it yourself.' While Justin said he hated just using a textbook during a discussion among a group of year 12 students in Perth (because 'You can't ask a textbook questions'), his classmate Colin said that was precisely how he liked to learn: 'I like textbooks, because the information's there and you can just learn it, like rote learning kind of stuff'.[48]

There's no doubt these students need to be catered for – they feel much more comfortable with a concrete, content-oriented history lesson. But I want to emphasis that they were a very small minority of the students I spoke with. For the most part, far from being undone by the challenge of multiple perspectives, students seemed to revel in the way they complicated the story of the past. In Canberra, Zoran thought that 'Discussions work best because you get different ideas flowing around using all the different people's perspectives.' In a group of year 12 students at a Melbourne public school, Melinda said she learns history best when her teacher 'put up a question on the board that everyone has to answer in a paragraph, and then she'll say, "Who wants to say something", and you'll get a lot of people put something in so you get a lot of different perspectives.' Her classmate Kaleb also likes 'Anything that shows two perspectives'.[49]

It wasn't just senior students who appreciated such complexity. Les, a year 10 student at a public school on the New South Wales Central Coast, said he 'loved' the subject 'because you can look at everything and there's no direct answer'.[50] In Tasmania, two year 10 students discussed what they enjoyed about learning history in similar terms:

> **Sally:** *And everyone has their own opinions about it. Everyone has their views on what happened, and that's good, because you sort of get different people's ideas, and you can work out what you think about it from other people's ideas.*
>
> **Allie:** *That's what I find interesting about it, like different people's opinions, and why they think that, rather than just facts being drilled into your brain.*[51]

Students have clear ideas about what makes an engaging history class. And in doing so (to my surprise, I admit) they offered quite complex understandings of the nature of the subject itself.

So where does this leave us? If the history classroom is where the subject dies or lives, these interviews give us a window into how students and teachers engage with Australia's past, or disengage from it, in the classroom. I think we're mad if we don't look in: while there's significant public concern about the state of young people's knowledge in Australia, we also know from their interviews that only teaching 'the facts' won't bring them any closer to the past. Students gave a pretty comprehensive list of the things that make Australian history seem dull, but they also gave a revealing lesson in what they find interesting. Kids enjoy history best when it comes alive in the classroom, and if we don't listen to that, what hope is there of generating lasting historical engagement?

Conclusion

> *I'd like every kid, whatever history lesson across the country, when they ask the question, 'Why are we doing this?', they get an answer. And I think if you can do that then the meaning of history will be realised.*

Brian, history teacher, New South Wales Central Coast

It's all too easy to think students don't know what's good for them: they hate school anyway, so why ask them how they learn? They think Australian history's boring, so why bother getting their opinions on the subject?

This wasn't the case for the students I spoke with. Sure, they were opinionated, critical and blunt (like many adolescents), but they engaged with the questions they were asked, and they had serious things to say about Australian history that deserve to be listened to. For too many students, Australian history is 'repetitive' or 'boring' or both. But is that their fault or ours?

Take federation. Students overwhelmingly acknowledged it was important to learn, but tracking down someone who enjoyed the topic was another matter. When I asked a group of year 10 students in Canberra how they found federation, Morgan was pretty dismissive: 'You do it lots of times,' she said, 'so you just get to know it after a while.' But doing it 'lots of times' hardly equates to historical engagement. Kate from Sydney thought that there needed to be 'a new way to sort of introduce it – not just the same way that you've probably heard like a million times – because once you start hearing about it again, you sort of switch off'.[1]

It's not just federation – topics such as Indigenous history or the goldrushes are just as likely to be taught and retaught without consistency. Many history classes learn patchy, repetitive versions of the past that chop and change between eras and events. There's no guarantee that students have any equivalent knowledge or historical understanding.

You certainly don't have to look very far to find worrying statistics that reveal how little 'our children' know about 'our nation's past', but headlines decrying kids' historical knowledge don't consider how they actually learn the subject. From the interviews it's pretty clear that while students understand the importance of Australian history, simply teaching them more facts more often won't bring them any closer to it.

Teachers are equally concerned about young people's knowledge of the past. But, like their students, they're not convinced more content is necessarily the answer. Amy, who teaches history in Canberra, feared any sort of approach to Australian history that would make it something 'they will *never* love'. Like many of his teaching colleagues, John from Sydney agreed that Australian history should be compulsory – as long as its complexity and interest were assured. 'Just how best to do it, I'm not sure of,' he said. 'I know that if it's too rigid, too chronologically structured, and it has to go all the way back to some specific point to work its way forward, it's sort of very mechanistic history.'[2]

In other words, there's no point teaching students Australian history without any engagement from *them* – and that means a curriculum which extends their knowledge and historical understanding, allows for discussion and debate, and connects kids to the past itself. These are the ideas that underlie concepts such as 'historical literacy' or 'historical understanding', where engaging students with the complexity of the subject is precisely what generates its interest and appeal.

This isn't just some fanciful academic argument: time and again in their focus groups around the country, students explained what they wanted from Australian history in these terms exactly. They acknowledge the importance of knowing the facts about Australian history, but they also want historical narratives, discussions and debates, and imagination in the classroom.

In Canberra, Rick liked learning history using 'a combination of approaches'. 'It's good to mix everything up just so you get different learning techniques,' he said. 'I mean, essays are always really good to learn in depth on one topic, but then discussions are good for general stuff, general knowledge.

Excursions always keep you interested because it's something different, something new – you're not in the classroom, you're out doing something else, so that helps you learn as well.'[3]

Ryan, a year 12 student in New South Wales, said he liked the fact that 'everyone's allowed to have their own opinions' in history. 'Like, you're allowed to have yours – I don't care – as long as you can kind of back up your evidence.' For Martin in Perth, engaging with different perspectives in class also made the subject interesting. 'I think history's all about viewpoints,' he said. But if 'you just write down notes on the board it's only one viewpoint, and kids are going to come and do a test on one viewpoint – so it's all going to be the same.'[4]

It got a bit dismal hearing student after student being so dismissive of Australian history. The subject is poorly co-ordinated, especially between primary and secondary schools, and students kept complaining that they'd 'done it' already. (And they probably *have* done it, but without any real depth or consistency.) A number of teachers I spoke with are also struggling with a lack of resources and even timetabling support within their own schools.

At the same time, it was also great to hear those examples of students and teachers enjoying the subject, and how they think it can be taught well. I simply wasn't expecting these two groups to have such similar thoughts about how to generate historical engagement: learning the facts is one aspect of understanding Australian history, they insisted; there's also the need to conduct research, to reconcile our present values with the actions and beliefs of people in the past, to understand how historical interpretations change over time, and to consider different points of view.

Brian from the Central Coast called it history's 'critical dimension': 'It's the idea of knowing it's okay to think critically,' he said. 'I just don't like the idea that there's an easy answer. My approach to history is taking the kid in there and immersing them in it and letting them enjoy it and think for themselves, as long as they can back it up intellectually. That to me is creating a citizen for the twenty-first century.'[5]

Curriculum officials were just as concerned to nurture students' historical skills. At the Department of Education in the Australian Capital Territory, Paul van Campenhout wanted students 'to know enough facts to be able to go on "Who Wants to be a Millionaire?" and know those key events,' he explained, 'but I also want a balance of the skills there, and that inquiry process as well – to actually go out and do the research on my own.'[6]

And the kids themselves? They also said that what they like about the subject is its capacity to go beyond core national knowledge. When I spoke with a group of students from a girls' school in Brisbane, Lily thought history was 'different to a subject like maths and stuff, because you can look at it and *interpret* it'. That interpretation 'may not be the same as the person next to you,' she said, 'but it doesn't mean it's wrong. So it's sort of more open for opinion as well.'[7] Like Lily, I'm convinced the subject is much more engaging and relevant when it's 'open for opinion'. And that means there has to be widespread recognition that history is something that we *do*, rather than just something that 'happened'.

The last thing kids want are teachers who 'are just doing it because they know they have to,' says Felicity, a year 10 student from Canberra. Or a classroom where the students are 'just looking at words and copying them down,' says Lily. 'They almost don't go into my head – they just go from my eyes to my notes.' Jeff goes to a Catholic boys' school in Brisbane and thinks the subject is more engaging 'with the student going out and being a proactive learner, rather than the teacher sort of feeding them information'.[8]

There's no doubt students sense that Australian history matters. 'With all the other subjects it's just like calculating, or writing,' explains Chen from Sydney, 'but in history you actually learn about your past, and we're living in history! So in fifty years time then we might be able to tell this to our children and grandchildren.' For Alana in Perth, the connection was just as strong: 'Yeah, I find, say, if I'm reading the paper now or something, and they'll talk about something that happened in the past I'll go, "oh I get that",' she said. 'Or they'll be talking about something that's linked today to what's happened in the past. And instead of going, "oh, alright", I actually understand what they're talking about.'[9]

The importance of Australian history isn't the main issue here – students already recognise this. They just ask that it be taught well.

Further reading

There are as many ways to teach history as there are school systems, curriculum documents and even teachers. So it's no surprise that the field of history education is characterised by a similarly broad range of approaches. While it's impossible to provide a comprehensive account of it all, I did want to highlight some of the key texts that have influenced my thinking on the topic, and provide a point of departure for those interested in further reading. Most of these sources have excellent and wide-ranging bibliographies of their own.

In the first instance, it might even be helpful to take a look at some discussions of national histories to get an idea of the fundamental questions that underlie the subject in schools. What is 'Australian history', for a start? What are the stories we tell ourselves, and what stories do we want to pass on to the next generation? Can we agree on them? Indeed, *should* we agree?

A number of studies, such as Lyn Spillman's *Nation and Commemoration: Creating National Identities in the United States and Australia* (Cambridge, Cambridge University Press, 1997) or Jeffrey Olick's *States of Memory: Continuities, Conflicts, and*

Transformations in National Retrospection (Durham; London, Duke University Press, 2003), examine how historical narratives shape and confirm national identity in challenging and complex ways. Benedict Anderson's much-cited text, *Imagined Communities: Reflections on the Origin and Spread of Nationalism* (London; New York, Verso, 1991), also explores how a sense of national identity emerges from the stories that are constructed around them.

It isn't just official types of 'public' commemorations that shape national affiliations – the ways people describe their own everyday historical connections are just as compelling. Roy Rosenzweig and David Thelen's remarkable research into Americans' historical sensibilities reveals deep and personal identifications with the past (*The Presence of the Past: Popular Uses of History in American Life*, New York, Columbia University Press, 1998). Paula Hamilton and Paul Ashton conducted a similar study in Australia, which confirmed the powerful (and varied) links people have with their family, community and national histories (see number 22 of *Australian Cultural History*, which was published as a special edition devoted to the project in 2003).

Yet it's difficult to move beyond the polarisation that has come to characterise debates over the past. Edward Linenthal and Tom Engelhardt's edited collection, *History Wars: The Enola Gay and Other Battles for the American Past* (New York, Metropolitan Books, 1996) examined outbreaks of these disputes – from the exhibition of the infamous Hiroshima bomber, the *Enola Gay*, at the Smithsonian Museum in Washington, to wider historical debates in the United States. James Davison Hunter's *Culture Wars: The Struggle to Define America* (New York, BasicBooks, 1991) provides a similarly contextual account of these public and political controversies that have consumed the country over the last twenty or thirty years.

Australia, too, has been at war in the historical sense.

During the Bicentenary in 1988, for example, there was significant disagreement over whether the anniversary should celebrate or commemorate the British colonisation of Australia. The 'black armband' debate the following decade cemented the adversarial lines of this public historical discussion. In 1993 Geoffrey Blainey introduced the term to describe what he felt had been a denigration of Australia's past (his Latham Lecture was published that year as 'Drawing Up a Balance Sheet of Our History' in *Quadrant* magazine, volume 37, numbers 7–8). Blainey sensed that an apologetic and overly mournful reading of the past had come to dominate much academic history writing, and the 'black armband' label gained popular currency. It even prompted some historians and commentators to respond that Blainey's reading of the past was coloured by his own 'white blindfold' – a historical dichotomy if ever there was!

Keith Windschuttle's claims that academic bias, rather than colonial violence, contributed to the number of Indigenous victims on Australia's frontier has generated the most recent round of the history wars (*The Fabrication of Aboriginal History: Vol. 1, Van Diemen's Land 1803–1847*, Sydney, Macleay Press, 2002). Robert Manne's edited collection *Whitewash: On Keith Windschuttle's Fabrication of Aboriginal History* (Melbourne, Black Inc., 2003) and Bain Attwood's *Telling the Truth about Aboriginal History* (Sydney, Allen & Unwin, 2005) responded critically to Windschuttle's assertions, and the debate has become more divisive than ever.

While I admit I'm a little uncomfortable with such dichotomous readings, they're hard to break out of. I contributed a chapter on history teaching to Stuart Macintyre's book *The History Wars* (Melbourne, Melbourne University Press, 2003). We were both hopeful the account would illuminate rather than confirm such historical divisions, but following its very politicised reception a few critics felt bound to disagree. For those interested in thinking about the nature of these historical debates, Ann Curthoys and John Docker's book, *Is History Fiction?*, gives a thoughtful and accessible discussion of how and why they keep recurring (Sydney, UNSW Press, 2006).

Teaching the nation's story in schools is as contested as any arena of the history wars and consumes historians, educationists and politicians alike. The deeply entrenched allegiances in these debates over history education prompted the American historian James Wertsch to ask in his excellent book, *Voices of Collective Remembering* (Cambridge, Cambridge University Press, 2002), to what extent contest over the subject really was about the nation's past or the politics of how that past is remembered?

Again, it's useful to look beyond Australia to get a sense of the dimensions of this debate. In Japan there have been long-standing disputes over the representation of its history in schoolbooks, which are periodically reported in the press here in Australia. The education board in Japan still censors history textbooks, and there have been continuing public controversies, even court cases, over the representation of Japanese wartime atrocities in the texts. Burton Bollag's article, 'A Confrontation With the Past: The Japanese Textbook Dispute', gives an in-depth account of this debate (and was published in 2001 in *American Educator*, volume 25, number 4). For an overview of Japanese historical commemoration, Ian Buruma's *The Wages of Guilt: Memories of War in Germany and Japan* (London, Vintage, 1995) and Laura Hein and Mark Seldon's edited collection, *Censoring History: Citizenship and Memory in Japan, Germany and the United States* (New York, ME Sharpe, 2000), also give excellent introductions to the ways in which Japan's legacy from World War II has been remembered.

When the United Kingdom was developing its own national curriculum in the late 1980s and early 1990s, there was heated political debate about what national heritage the curriculum should be presenting: the Conservative Government was convinced that current history curricula didn't contain enough strong, positive national images; many historians and teachers, meanwhile, questioned the political motivations behind the Tory critique. The episode has many resonances here in Australian debates about a compulsory national curriculum, and it's worth reading Robert Phillips' book, *History Teaching, Nationhood and the State: A Study in Educational Politics* (London, Cassell, 1998) to get a sense of these recurring curriculum concerns.

Debate was also intractable in the United States over the development of national history standards, generating another flurry of academic writing on the politics of history education. Upon their release in 1994, the standards were criticised by a number of conservative politicians, educationists and media commentators for their apparent political correctness. History standards should cement the proud place of American history, they determined, rather than question it. A number of studies document the heated toing and froing of this debate, and provide a fascinating account of how it unfolded. Linda Symcox's book, *Whose History? The Struggle for National Standards in American Classrooms* (New York, Teachers College Press, 2002), catalogues all the major parties and views. The authors of the standards (Gary Nash, Charlotte Crabtree and Ross Dunn) also produced a response of their own, which strongly defended their pedagogical and historical approach (*History on Trial: Culture Wars and the Teaching of the Past,* New York, Alfred A. Knopf, 1997).

In Australia, similar debates have unfolded about what history to teach, and how to teach it. Should history be taught as a stand-alone subject or within amalgamated studies such as SOSE? Do we need a centralised national curriculum, or should each state and territory develop and co-ordinate its own particular approach to the past? In 1998 the historian

Alan Ryan published an article in the *Bulletin* of the Australian Historical Association titled 'Developing a Strategy to "Save" History', which lamented the decline of the subject in Australian schools (*AHA Bulletin*, number 87). Ryan's concern was confirmed by research conducted in the 1990s, such as the survey results published in the Civics Expert Group's report 'Whereas the People ... Civics and Citizenship Education' (Canberra, Commonwealth of Australia, 1994), which revealed worryingly low levels of national historical knowledge among Australian schoolchildren.

But the answer wasn't clear by any means. While many agreed with Ryan that something drastic had to be done, others defended the subject in schools. In the following two issues of the *Bulletin* (numbers 88 and 89), teachers, historians and educationists responded in droves to Ryan's original article, and they provide a lively professional forum about the status of history teaching in Australia that's worth revisiting.

There has been a real political and pedagogical tussle over the way Australian history should be taught in schools. Alan Barcan's lengthy piece, 'History in Decay', was published in *Quadrant* magazine (volume 43, numbers 7–8) in 1999, and insisted that a retreat from traditional history was irrevocably damaging the subject in schools. (Keith Windschuttle had made similar charges about academic history in his book, *The Killing of History*, Sydney, Macleay Press, 1994.) More recently, Kevin Donnelly's work has also galvanised conservative opinion against progressive forms of history education. His books, *Why Our Schools are Failing* (Sydney, Duffy & Snellgrove, 2004) and *Dumbing Down* (Melbourne, Hardie Grant Books, 2007), as well as many newspaper columns, argue for a return to traditional, content-oriented curricula and teaching practices. These defenders of traditional approaches to the subject invoke concerns expressed by American educationists such as Diane

Ravitch and ED Hirsch against multicultural, postmodern and politically correct readings of the past.

Despite the influence of conservative commentators, it's unwise to read an over-arching political divide into this educational debate. (It isn't nearly so simple as the left–right dichotomy implied by terms such as the 'history wars'.) After all, it was a Labor premier, Bob Carr, who rejected the adoption of SOSE in New South Wales in favour of mandatory Australian history. And there are plenty of political conservatives – some who attended the 2006 Australian History Summit – who insist that no Australian history curriculum should be conceived at the expense of classroom engagement or student interest.

To get a sense of the complexity of these debates, it's worthwhile taking a look at some of the journals from History Teachers' Associations around Australia. *Agora* (Victoria), *Teaching History* (New South Wales), *The History Teacher* (Queensland) and the *Australian History Teacher* from the History Teachers' Association of Australia, have collections that go back to the 1960s and 70s, and provide a comprehensive record of the sorts of issues – both curricular and classroom – that teachers and historians have engaged with in Australia.

On the issue of teaching and learning in particular, there's increasingly accessible research available. In the United Kingdom, Rosalyn Ashby and Peter Lee have continued to develop approaches to history teaching that take into account the ways students learn the subject. Lee and Ashby's research builds on the British School Council's History 13–16 Project from the 1970s. They advocate teaching complex ideas about history in school and insist that students themselves are more than capable of dealing with them.

The work of North American history educationists such as Sam Wineburg and Peter Seixas also delves into the process of historical understanding. How do students learn to think historically? Can they deal with multiple perspectives, or is the purpose of history education to give a more concrete foundation of the nation's past? In his book, *Historical Thinking and Other Unnatural Acts* (Philadelphia, Temple University Press, 2001), Wineburg argues that understanding history is by no means intuitive and must be taught in all its complexity to be taught well. Peter Seixas's work on historical consciousness also studies how historical understanding is developed. His edited volumes, *Theorizing Historical Consciousness* (Toronto, University of Toronto Press, 2006) and (with Peter Stearns and Sam Wineburg) *Knowing, Teaching and Learning History: National and International Perspectives* (New York and London, New York University Press, 2000), are impressive collections on contemporary history education.

Such research on how children learn history, and how it should be taught, guides much of the academic discussion about the subject. But in Australia at least, gauging students' attitudes to their nation's past has been rather more sporadic. The History Teachers' Association published a report by Christine Halse on history teaching in New South Wales in 1997, which includes lively interview material from teachers and students on the state of the subject there. Ashton and Hamilton's *Australians and the Past* study included some interviews with history teachers. Tony Taylor's National Inquiry into School History from 2000 also drew on focus group interviews with teachers around the country (see: <http://www.dest.gov.au/sectors/school_education/publications_resources/profiles/school_history.htm>. And in 2004 the History Council of New South Wales published *A Future for the Past: The State of Children's History*, a small collection of papers from a symposium on history teaching. Bruce Scates' introduction includes a couple of lovely excerpts from students' presentations on the day. Another piece by Julie Edwards on the historical attitudes of some Victorian students was published in 2005, and provides some excellent material from her interviews ('Researching the

Development of Historical Consciousness in Late Primary and Junior Secondary Students', *Curriculum Perspectives*, volume 25, number 1).

This appendix isn't a complete list of supplementary reading – typing 'history teaching' into a newspaper database alone will generate hundreds of possible articles. And there are many other fields that may be of interest, such as cognitive psychology, history textbooks, or curriculum development. But I've found the texts presented here to be useful and engaging, and this short discussion reflects much of my thinking on the topic. I hope it gives some ideas for further study.

Notes

All interview transcriptions and notes are in possession of the author.

Introduction

1 Ministerial Council on Education, Employment, Training and Youth Affairs, 'Civics and Citizenship Years 6 and 10 Report 2004' (Melbourne, Curriculum Corporation, 2006), <http://www.mceetya.edu.au/verve/_resources/Civics_and_Citizenship_Years_6_10_Report.pdf>, p. 35; Tony Taylor, 'Disputed Territory: Some Political Contexts for the Development of Australian Historical Consciousness' (paper presented at the Canadian Historical Consciousness in an International Context: Theoretical Frameworks conference, University of British Columbia, Vancouver, BC, 2001), <http://www.cshc.ubc.ca/pwias/viewabstract.php?7>.
2 *Prime Minister John Howard's address to the National Press Club on January 25, 2006*, <http://theage.com.au/news/national/pms-speech/2006/01/25/1138066849045.html?page=fullpage contentSwap1>.
3 Australian Broadcasting Corporation, '7.30 Report', 26 January 2006, <http://www.abc.net.au/7.30/content/2006/s1556052.htm>. For some of the public comment, have a look at any of the major Australian newspapers in the week following the Prime Minister's speech. For example: Janet Albrechtsen, 'Textbook case of making our past a blame game', *The Australian*, 1 February 2006; Kevin Donnelly, 'Why our greatest story is just not being told', *The Australian*, 28 January

2006; Michelle Grattan, 'PM claims victory in culture wars', *The Age*, 26 January 2006; Michael Harvey, 'PM wants new history', *Herald-Sun*, 26 January 2006; Samantha Maiden, 'Howard wants history back', *The Australian*, 26 January 2006; Peter Ruehl, 'Historical oblivion won't fly', *Australian Financial Review*, 28 January 2006; Imre Salusinszky, 'History debate rages over loss of narrative', *The Australian*, 27 January 2006; Luke Slattery, 'PM accused of narrow view of history', *Australian Financial Review*, 27 January 2006; Andrew West, 'Bad history: blame John Howard' (online discussion), *Sydney Morning Herald*, 31 January 2006, <http://blogs.smh.com.au/thecontrarian/archives/2006/01/bad_history_i_b.html>.

4 Farrah Tomazin, 'Schools "neglecting" war history', *The Age*, 17 April 2006; Neil Wilson, 'Teach kids about war', *Herald-Sun*, 11 November 2004.

5 See: David Kennedy, '1988 ban a matter of history, say teachers', *Sydney Morning Herald*, 8 January 1988; For conservative commentary on 1988, see: Ken Baker, 'The Bicentenary: Celebration or Apology?' *IPA Review* (Summer 1985), pp. 175–82; John Hirst, 'The Blackening of Our Past', *IPA Review* (December–February 1988/89), pp. 49–54; Hugh Morgan, 'The Guilt Industry', *IPA Review* (May–July 1988), pp. 17–20; Geoffrey Partington, 'Education for Citizenship in Bicentennial Australia', *Quadrant*, vol. 32, no. 8 (1988), pp. 29–35; Geoffrey Partington, 'History Teaching in Bicentennial Australia', *Forum* (HTASA) (December 1987), pp. 17–35. And for a history teacher perspective, see: Bob Lewis, 'The Bicentenary – What is the Role of the HTAV?' *Agora*, vol. 22, no. 4 (1987), pp. 11–13.

6 Tony Hewett, 'Students reject 200th medals', *Sydney Morning Herald*, 10 May 1988; Anne Susskind, 'More 200th medals returned', *Sydney Morning Herald*, 18 May 1988.

7 John Carroll (with Richard Longes Carroll, Philip Jones & Patricia Vickers-Rich), 'Review of the National Museum of Australia, its exhibitions and public programs: a report to the Council of the National Museum of Australia' (Canberra, Department of Communications, Information Technology and the Arts, 2003), <http://www.nma.gov.au/shared/libraries/attachments/review/review_report_20030715/files/552/ReviewReport20030715.pdf>. See also: Stuart Macintyre & Anna Clark, *The History Wars* (Melbourne, Melbourne University Press, 2003), chapter 10; Keith Windschuttle, 'Exposing academic deception of past wrongs', *Sydney Morning Herald*, 19 September 2000; Keith Windschuttle, *The Fabrication of Aboriginal History: Vol. 1, Van Diemen's Land 1803–1847* (Sydney, Macleay, 2002); ed. Robert Manne, *Whitewash: On Keith Windschuttle's Fabrication of Aboriginal History* (Melbourne, Black Inc., 2003).

8 Anna Clark, *Teaching the Nation: Politics and Pedagogy in Australian*

History (Melbourne, Melbourne University Press, 2006), chapter 1; Ray Land, '"Furore over Invasion Text": Introduction to the Politics Process and Players', in *Invasion and After: A Case Study in Curriculum Politics*, ed. Ray Land (Griffith University, Queensland Studies Centre, 1994), pp. 1–11.

9 Jenny Lawless, Inspector for Human Society in Its Environment (including History), New South Wales Board of Studies, 24 August 2006.

10 Stuart Macintyre, 'The Genie and the Bottle: Putting History Back into the School Curriculum', *Australian Journal of Education*, vol. 41, no. 2 (1997), pp. 189–98; Alan Ryan, 'In Defence of "Disciplinism"', *AHA Bulletin*, no. 89 (1999), pp. 11–14; Tony Taylor, 'Too many cooks spoil the SOSE', *The Age*, 7 May 2007. And for media comment, see: Editorial, 'An educated change', *The Australian*, 26 April 2007 <http://www.theaustralian.news.com.au/story/0,20867,21620958-7583,00.html>; Editorial, 'Trouble with syllabus is fundamental', *Courier Mail*, 2 September 2000.

11 'The Future of Schooling in Australia' (Melbourne, Council for the Australian Federation, 2007), <http://www.dpc.vic.gov.au/CA256D800027B102/Lookup/FederalistPaper2TheFutureofSchoolinginAustralia/$file/Federalist%20Paper%202%20The%20Future%20of%20Schooling%20in%20Australia.pdf>.

12 *History Years 7–10 Syllabus* (Sydney, New South Wales Board of Studies, 2003); *Studies of Society and Environment: Years 1–10 Syllabus (with Years 9 and 10 optional subject syllabuses)* (Brisbane, Queensland School Curriculum Council, 2000).

13 Paul Ashton & Paula Hamilton, 'At Home with the Past: Background and Initial Findings from the National Survey', *Australian Cultural History*, no. 22 (2003), pp. 5–30.

14 Frustrated with the level of debate over national historical knowledge in the USA, the history educationist Sam Wineburg asked this very question in his influential collection on the topic: 'It may be that we have spent so much time discovering (only to rediscover over and over and over ...) what students *don't* know that we have neglected more useful questions about young people's historical knowledge. For example, what *do* students know about the past?' Sam Wineburg, *Historical Thinking and Other Unnatural Acts: Charting the Future of Teaching the Past* (Philadelphia, Temple University Press, 2001), p. vii.

15 Only two of the teacher interviews were conducted in groups (as almost all of the teachers were the sole representatives from their school). Interviews with curriculum officials were equally divided between group interviews with curriculum teams and individual curriculum designers.

16   In those states and territories where history is taught within Studies of Society and Environment (SOSE), some of the teachers I interviewed considered themselves SOSE teachers, rather than just history teachers. Since they teach history within SOSE, and this project compares the teaching and learning of Australian history nationally, I refer to them as 'history teachers' in the text.
17   Australian Bureau of Statistics, 'Report 4221.0: 2006 Schools (Australia)' (Canberra, Australian Bureau of Statistics, 2007), pp. 11, 25, < http://www.ausstats.abs.gov.au/ausstats/subscriber.nsf/0/ 9DDA83611950C66FCA25728B000CFC92/$File/42210_2006.pdf>.
18   Catriona Jackson, 'Academic condemns history teaching', *Canberra Times*, 4 June 2001.
19   'Tamsyn', history teacher, public high school, Canberra, 18 August 2006; 'Elizabeth', former history teacher, Canberra, 18 August 2006.
20   'Zoran', public senior college, Canberra, 18 August 2006.
21   'Pia', public girls' high school, Sydney, 21 August 2006; 'Trace', public high school, Brisbane, 26 July 2006.
22   'Jake', public high school, Brisbane, 25 July 2006.
23   Interview with students, public high school, Darwin, 21 June 2006.
24   Interview with students, independent Islamic college, Sydney, 23 August 2006.
25   'Cameron', Catholic boys' school, Perth, 23 May 2006; 'Stephanie', public high school, Hobart, 3 May 2006.
26   'Brian', history teacher, New South Wales Central Coast, 22 August 2006.
27   Judith Brett & Anthony Moran, *Ordinary People's Politics* (Melbourne, Pluto Press, 2006), p. 4.
28   Keith C Barton & Linda S Levstik, *Teaching History for the Common Good* (Mahwah, NJ, Lawrence Erlbaum Associates, Inc., 2004), p. 14.

Chapter 1

1   'Jeff', Catholic boys' school, Brisbane, 25 July 2006; 'Keira', public high school, Northern Territory (near Darwin), 22 June 2006.
2   'Alex', public high school, Adelaide, 13 June 2006; 'Amber', public senior college, Canberra, 18 August 2006.
3   'Mary', history teacher, public high school, Brisbane, 26 July 2006; 'Ellen', history teacher, public high school, Darwin, 21 June 2006.
4   Civics Expert Group, 'Whereas the people ... Civics and Citizenship Education' (Canberra, Commonwealth of Australia, 1994), pp. 3, 10, 50, 143; Murray Print, 'Political Understanding and Attitudes of Secondary Students' (Canberra, Parliamentary Education Office, 1995), pp. 3, 13, 39–40.
5   Cited in Taylor, Tony Taylor, 'Disputed Territory: Some Political

Contexts for the Development of Australian Historical Consciousness' (paper presented at the Canadian Historical Consciousness in an International Context: Theoretical Frameworks conference, University of British Columbia, Vancouver, BC, 2001), <http://www.cshc.ubc.ca/pwias/viewabstract.php?7>.

6   See, for example, a 2006 report prepared for the Ministerial Council on Education, Employment, Training and Youth Affairs by the Australian Council of Education Research which revealed that the vast majority of Australian teenagers did not know Australia Day commemorated the arrival of the First Fleet, and most were also ignorant of the reason for Anzac Day: Ministerial Council on Education, Employment, Training and Youth Affairs, 'Civics and Citizenship Years 6 and 10 Report 2004' (Melbourne, Curriculum Corporation, 2006), <http://www.mceetya.edu.au/verve/_resources/Civics_and_Citizenship_Years_6_10_Report.pdf>.
7   Julie Beare, 'Letter', Adelaide *Advertiser*, 8 May 1999; Ross Fitzgerald, 'Letter', *Courier-Mail*, 4 September 2000.
8   Tony Taylor & Carmel Young, 'Making History: A Guide for the Teaching and Learning of History in Australian Schools' (Canberra, Department of Education, Science and Training, 2003), p. 15, <http://www.hyperhistory.org/index.php?option=displaypage&Itemid=630&op=page>.
9   'John', history teacher, public girls' high school, Sydney, 21 August 2006; 'Sarah', history teacher, independent girls' school, Melbourne, 11 April 2006.
10 Kim Sweetman, 'FEDERAL BUDGET '95 History and government course to target all ages', Adelaide *Advertiser*, 10 May 1995; Stephanie Raethel, 'Canberra sets politics for years 4–10', *Sydney Morning Herald*, 9 May 1997; David Kemp, 'Media Release: History Takes Centre Stage' (Canberra, David Kemp Media Release K192) 15 October 2000, <http://www.dest.gov.au/archive/ministers/kemp/oct00/k0192_151000.htm>.
11 'Marco', history teacher, public high school, outer Melbourne, 16 May 2006.
12 'Sally', history teacher, public high school, central Victoria, 6 April 2006.
13 'Neil', history teacher, public senior college, Canberra, 18 August 2006.
14 'Daniel', history teacher, Catholic boys' school, Brisbane, 25 July 2006; 'Elizabeth', former history teacher, Canberra, 18 August 2006.
15 'Emma', public high school, Hobart, 3 May 2006; 'Morgan', independent girls' school, Canberra, 17 August 2006.
16 Interview with students, public K–10 school, south-eastern Tasmania, 4 May 2006.

17 'Gail', history teacher, public K–10 school, south-eastern Tasmania, 4 May 2006.
18 'Justine', history teacher, public high school, central Australia, 16 June 2006.
19 'Lydia', independent co-educational school, Adelaide, 14 June 2006.
20 Interview with students, public senior college, Canberra, 18 August 2006; Interview with students, public senior college, Perth, 25 May 2006.
21 Christine Halse, et al., 'The State of History in New South Wales' (Sydney, History Teachers' Association of New South Wales, 1997); Tony Taylor, 'Future of the Past – Final Report of the National Inquiry into School History' (Canberra, Department of Education, Training and Youth Affairs, 2000), <http://www.dest.gov.au/sectors/school_education/publications_resources/national_inquiry_into_school_history/the_future_of_the_past_final_report.htm>; Tony Taylor with Anna Clark, 'An overview of the teaching and learning of Australian history in schools: prepared for the Australian History Summit, Canberra, August 17th 2006' (Canberra, Department of Education, Science and Training, 2006), <http://www.dest.gov.au/NR/rdonlyres/46FC0B32-702B-4D93-99BA-E25F30621625/13382/HistorySummit_DESTMapping_004FINALtotal.pdf>.
22 'Sal', public high school, Perth, 22 May August 2006; 'Kate', public girls' high school, Sydney, 21 August 2006.
23 Interview with students, public high school, Darwin, 21 June 2006.
24 Interview with students, Catholic boys' school, Adelaide, 15 June 2006.
25 'Kate', public girls' high school, Sydney, 21 August 2006.
26 Interview with students, independent girls' school, Canberra, 17 August 2006.
27 'Arthur', Catholic boys' school, Brisbane, 25 July 2006; 'Nada', independent Islamic school, Sydney, 23 August 2006.
28 Julie Bishop, 'Our classrooms need to make a date with the facts', *The Australian*, 6 July 2006.
29 'Neil', history teacher, public senior college, Canberra, 18 August 2006.
30 'Tamsyn', history teacher, public high school, Canberra, 18 August 2006.
31 'Elouise', history teacher, independent girls' school, Perth, 24 May 2006.
32 Tony Brian-Davis, history teacher and former manager, Commonwealth History Project, 13 June 2006.
33 'Miranda', public high school, Brisbane, 25 July 2006.
34 Interview with students, Catholic boys' school, Brisbane, 25 July 2006.
35 'Deborah', history teacher, public senior college, Canberra, 18 August 2006.

36 'Brian', history teacher, public high school, New South Wales Central Coast, 22 August 2006.
37 'Stephanie', history teacher, public high school, Hobart, 3 May 2006; 'Sandra', history teacher, public senior college, Perth, 24 May 2006.
38 'Caitlin', independent girls' school, Melbourne, 11 April 2006; 'Morgan', independent girls' school, Canberra, 17 August 2006.
39 Interview with students, public high school, Darwin, 21 June 2006.
40 Interview with students, public high school, Brisbane, 25 July 2006.
41 'Les', public high school, New South Wales Central Coast, 22 August 2006.
42 Ministerial Council on Education, Employment, Training and Youth Affairs 'Civics and Citizenship Years 6 and 10 Report 2004'; Jewel Topsfield, 'Howard attacks "fad" schooling', *The Age*, 9 February 2006.

Chapter 2

1 Farrah Tomazin, 'From war zone to war homage: student honours the digger spirit', *The Age*, 17 April 2006.
2 'Ramah', independent Islamic school, Sydney, 23 August 2006.
3 'John', history teacher, public girls' school, Sydney, 21 August 2006.
4 'Robert', Catholic boys' school, Perth, 23 May 2006.
5 Interview with students, public senior college, Canberra, 18 August 2006; 'Ryan', public high school, New South Wales Central Coast, 22 August 2006.
6 Bruce Scates, 'Walking with History: School Excursions to the Cemeteries of the Great War', in *A Future for the Past: The State of Children's History*, ed. Bruce Scates (Sydney, History Council of New South Wales, 2004), p. 93; Bruce Scates, *Return to Gallipoli: Walking the Battlefields of the Great War* (Melbourne, Cambridge University Press, 2006).
7 'Brendan', Catholic boys' school, Brisbane, 25 July 2006; 'Declan', Catholic boys' school, Adelaide, 15 June 2006.
8 'Morgan', independent girls' school, Canberra, 17 August 2006; 'Julia', public high school, Hobart, 3 May 2006; Interview with students, independent co-educational school, Hobart, 3 May 2006.
9 'Greg', history teacher, independent girls' school, Brisbane, 24 July 2006. 'Michael', history teacher, public high school, southern New South Wales, 20 July 2006.
10 John Firth, Chief Executive Officer, Victorian Curriculum and Assessment Authority, 13 May 2006.
11 Paul Ashton & Paula Hamilton, 'At Home with the Past: Background and Initial Findings from the National Survey', *Australian Cultural History*, no. 22 (2003), pp. 5–30; Graeme Davison, 'The Habit of

Commemoration and the Revival of Anzac Day', *Australian Cultural History*, no. 22 (2003), pp. 77–81.

12 Historians such as Marilyn Lake and Clare Wright claim that our current political climate has in fact enshrined a conservative commemoration of our past. 'John Howard's efforts to militarise Australian historical memory', Lake suggests, has pushed war anniversaries to the fore of our national calendar: Marilyn Lake, 'The Militarisation of Australia's Historical Memory', *Teaching History*, vol. 40, no. 1, March 2006, pp. 15–16. Marilyn Lake, 'The Howard history of Australia', *The Age*, 20 August 2005; Clare Wright, 'Placing the answer before the question betrays a closed mind', *The Age*, 13 September 2006.

13 'Stephen', history teacher, Catholic boys' school, Adelaide, 15 June 2006; 'Elouise', history teacher, independent girls' school, Perth, 24 May 2006.

14 'Michael', history teacher, public high school, southern New South Wales, 20 July 2006.

15 'Marco', history teacher, public high school, outer Melbourne, 16 May 2006; 'Stephanie', history teacher, public high school, Hobart, 3 May 2006.

16 Interview with students, independent girls' school, Perth, 24 May 2006. For a discussion of the role of Anzac Day in contemporary Australia, see: Irving Saulwick, cited in Davison, 'The Habit of Commemoration and the Revival of Anzac Day', *Australian Cultural History*, no. 22 (2003), p. 80.

17 Editorial, 'An uneducated guess about school values', *The Age*, 22 January 2004.

18 Editorial, 'An uneducated guess about school values'; Chee Chee Leung, Orietta Guerrera, with Annabel Crabb, 'Private, public teachers hit PM', *The Age*, 21 January 2004; Mark Riley, Linda Doherty & Kelly Burke, 'PM's attack on public schools ignites anger', *Sydney Morning Herald*, 21 January 2004.

19 'Values Education Study Final Report' (Melbourne, Curriculum Corporation, 2003); 'A Draft National Framework for Values Education in Australian Schools' (Canberra, Department of Education, Science and Training, 2004); Andrew Fraser, 'Parents fly the way on poles', *Canberra Times*, 29 June 2004; John Howard & Brendan Nelson, 'Media Release: The Australian Government's Agenda for Schools – Achievement Through Choice and Opportunity' (Canberra, Brendan Nelson Media Centre, 2004), <http://www.dest.gov.au/ministers/nelson/jun_04/npm_220604.htm>.

20 Australian Broadcasting Corporation, *ABC Online Forum*, 23 June 2004, <http://www2b.abc.net.au/news/forum/newsonline1/archives/archive29/default.shtm>.

21 Adrian Wilson, 'Letter', *The Age*, 24 June 2004; Polly Price, 'Letter', *Sydney Morning Herald*, 1 July 2004; Matthew Pinkney, 'PM's jelly bean politics', *Herald-Sun*, 28 June 2004.
22 Samantha Hawley, 'Brendan Nelson addresses Islamic schools on Australian values', 'The World Today', 24 August 2005, <http://www.abc.net.au/worldtoday/content/2005/s1445094.htm>; Samantha Hawley, 'Teach Australian values or "clear off", says Nelson', 'PM', 24 August 2005, <http://www.abc.net.au/pm/content/2005/s1445262.htm>; Ben Haywood, 'Battlelines drawn on values', *The Age*, 4 September 2005.
23 Interview with students, public high school, Darwin, 21 June 2006.
24 Interview with students, independent girls' school, Perth, 24 May 2006.
25 John Howard, 'The Liberal Tradition: The Beliefs and Values Which Guide the Federal Government', *1996 Sir Robert Menzies Lecture* (18 November 1996); cited in Michelle Grattan, 'Accept Australian values or get out, Nelson declares', *The Age*, 25 August 2005.
26 Lillian Saleh, 'We are good Aussies – Muslim schools defend the values they teach', *Daily Telegraph*, 25 August 2005; cited in Hawley, 'Brendan Nelson addresses Islamic schools on Australian values'.
27 'Elouise', history teacher, independent girls' school, Perth, 24 May 2006.
28 Interview with students, Catholic boys' school, Brisbane, 25 July 2006.
29 Interview with students, independent girls' school, Canberra, 17 August 2006.
30 'Ophelia', co-educational independent school, Adelaide, 14 June 2006.
31 'Cameron', history teacher, Catholic boys' school, Perth, 23 May 2006.
32 'Lara', history teacher, public high school, Adelaide, 13 June 2006; 'Andrew', history teacher, independent co-educational school, Hobart, 3 May 2006.
33 'Tanya', history teacher, public high school, Northern Territory (near Darwin), 22 June 2006; 'Greg', history teacher, independent girls' school, Brisbane, 24 July 2006.
34 Interview with students, independent girls' school, Brisbane, 24 July 2006.
35 'Felicity', independent girls' school, Canberra, 17 August 2006.
36 Interview with students, independent Islamic school, Sydney, 23 August 2006.
37 Janine Giles, Western Australian Curriculum Council, Perth, 22 May 2006.
38 Interview with students, public senior college, Perth, 24 May 2006.
39 Interview with students, public high school, New South Wales Central Coast, 22 August 2006.

40 'Jessica' history teacher, public high school, Brisbane, 25 July 2006.
41 Jan Bishop, former history teacher, Perth, 23 May 2006.

Chapter 3

1 'Marco', history teacher, public high school, outer Melbourne, 16 May 2006; 'Deborah', history teacher, senior secondary college, Canberra, 18 August 2006.
2 'Emma', public high school, Hobart, 3 May 2006; 'Sophia', public high school, Adelaide, 13 June 2006.
3 Interview with students, public high school, Brisbane, 26 July 2006.
4 Interview with students, public high school, Brisbane, 25 July 2006.
5 Interview with students, independent girls' school, Brisbane, 24 July 2006.
6 'Megan', independent girls' school, Perth, 24 May 2006.
7 Interview with students, public high school, Brisbane, 25 July 2006.
8 'Natalie', public high school, Darwin, 21 June 2006; 'Declan', Catholic boys' school, Adelaide, 15 June 2006; 'Trace', public high school, Brisbane, 25 July 2006.
9 'Tamsyn', history teacher, public high school, Canberra, 18 August 2006; 'Lara', history teacher, public high school, Adelaide, 13 June 2006; 'Sarah', history teacher, independent girls' school, Melbourne, 11 April 2006.
10 'Les', public high school, New South Wales Central Coast, 22 August 2006.
11 Brian, history teacher, public high school, New South Wales Central Coast, 22 August 2006; 'Mary', history teacher, public high school, Brisbane, 26 July 2006.
12 'Samantha', independent girls' school, Melbourne, 11 April 2006.
13 'Neil', history teacher, public senior college, Canberra, 18 August 2006.
14 'Elizabeth', former history teacher, Canberra, 18 August 2006.
15 John Howard, 'Weekly House Hansard, 30 October 1996' (Canberra, Australia, House of Representatives, 1996), 6158; John Howard, 'The Liberal Tradition: The Beliefs and Values Which Guide the Federal Government', *1996 Sir Robert Menzies Lecture* (18 November 1996).
16 'Adrian', Catholic boys' school, Brisbane, 25 July 2006.
17 Judith Brett, 'Relaxed and Comfortable: The Liberal Party's Australia', *Quarterly Essay*, no. 19 (2005).
18 Interview with students, independent girls' school, Perth, 24 May 2006.
19 Try, for example, *Teaching History* (NSW), *History Teacher* (Queensland), *Agora* (Victoria) or the national journal, the *Australian History Teacher*.

20 Julie Fisher, Principal Education Officer, Studies of Society and Environment, Tasmanian Department of Education, Hobart, 6 May 2006.
21 Henry Reynolds, *Why Weren't We Told? A Personal Search for the Truth about Our History* (Ringwood, Viking, 1998), p. 133.
22 'Kylie', student teacher, University of Sydney, 18 August 2007.
23 Terry Woolley, Executive Director of Primary, Middle and Senior Secondary Services, South Australian Department of Education and Children's Services, Adelaide, 15 June 2006.
24 Portus writes that after years of racial violence on the frontier, 'the killing-off policy was abandoned, and the last days of the dying race are being passed in a better atmosphere of mercy and succour from their white brethren': GV Portus, *Australia Since 1606*, 2nd ed. (Melbourne, Oxford University Press, 1955), p. 158.
25 'Michael', history teacher, public high school, southern New South Wales, 20 July 2006.
26 'Greg', history teacher, independent girls' school, Brisbane, 24 July 2006.
27 'Sarah', history teacher, independent girls' school, Melbourne, 11 April 2006.
28 Tony Taylor with Anna Clark, 'An Overview of the Teaching and Learning of Australian History in Schools: Prepared for the Australian History Summit, Canberra, August 17th 2006' (Canberra, Department of Education, Science and Training, 2006), <http://www.dest.gov.au/NR/rdonlyres/46FC0B32-702B-4D93-99BA-E25F30621625/13382/HistorySummit_DESTMapping_004FINALtotal.pdf>, pp. 33, 34.
29 *History Years 7–10 Syllabus* (Sydney, New South Wales Board of Studies, 2003), <http://www.boardofstudies.nsw.edu.au/syllabus_sc/pdf_doc/history_710_syl.pdf>, 26; *Human Society and its Environment K–6* (Sydney, New South Wales Board of Studies, 2006), <http://k6.boardofstudies.nsw.edu.au/files/hsie/k6_hsie_syl.pdf>.
30 *Studies of Society and Environment: Years 1–10 Syllabus (with Years 9 and 10 optional subject syllabuses)* (Brisbane, Queensland School Curriculum Council, 2000), <http://www.qsa.qld.edu.au/yrs1to10/kla/sose/docs/syllabus/options.pdf>, p. 8; *South Australian Curriculum, Standards and Accountability Framework: Middle Years Band* (Adelaide, Department of Education, Training and Employment, 2001), <http://www.sacsa.sa.edu.au/index_fsrc.asp?t=Home>, p. 315.
31 *Studies of Society and Environment: Years 1–10 Syllabus (with Years 9 and 10 optional subject syllabuses)* (Brisbane, Queensland School Curriculum Council, 2000), <http://www.qsa.qld.edu.au/yrs1to10/kla/sose/docs/syllabus/options.pdf>, p. 8; *South Australian Curriculum, Standards and Accountability Framework: Middle Years Band* (Adelaide, Department of Education, Training and Employment 2001), <http://www.sacsa.sa.edu.au/index_fsrc.asp?t=Home>, p. 315.

32 *Studies of Society and Environment: Years 1–10 Syllabus (with Years 9 and 10 optional subject syllabuses)* (Queensland), p. 39.
33 'Lee', public senior college, Canberra, 18 August 2006.
34 'Neil', history teacher, public senior college, Canberra, 18 August 2006.
35 'John', history teacher, public girls' high school, Sydney, 21 August 2006.
36 'Susan', student teacher, University of Sydney, 18 August 2007; 'Tamsyn', history teacher, public high school, Canberra, 18 August 2006.
37 'Justine', history teacher, public high school, central Australia, 16 June 2006.
38 'David', history teacher, public high school, central Australia, 20 June 2006.
39 'Tanya', history teacher, public high school, Northern Territory (near Darwin), 22 June 2006.
40 'Gabby', public high school, Darwin, 21 June 2006.
41 'Mary', history teacher, public high school, Brisbane, 26 July 2006; 'Jessica', history teacher, public high school, Brisbane, 25 July 2006.
42 'Greg', history teacher, independent girls' school, Brisbane, 24 July 2006; 'Brian', history teacher, public high school, New South Wales Central Coast, 22 August 2006.
43 'Sam', co-educational independent school, Adelaide, 14 June 2006; Interview with students, public high school, Hobart, 4 May 2006.
44 'Esme', public high school, Melbourne, 30 March 2006.
45 Interview with students, public high school, Brisbane, 25 July 2006.
46 'Mal', history teacher, public high school, Northern Territory (near Darwin), 22 June 2006.
47 'Ellen', history teacher, public high school, Darwin, 21 June 2006.
48 'Annie', independent girls' school, Canberra, 17 August 2006; 'Allie', independent co-educational school, Hobart, 3 May 2006; 'Ellen', history teacher, public high school, Darwin, 21 June 2006.
49 Interview with students, independent girls' school, Canberra, 17 August 2006;
50 *History Extension Stage 6 Syllabus* (Sydney, New South Wales Board of Studies, 1999), <http://www.boardofstudies.nsw.edu.au/syllabus_hsc/pdf_doc/historyext_syl.pdf>.
51 'Marco', history teacher, public high school, outer Melbourne, 16 May 2006.
52 'Janice', history teacher, co-educational independent school, Adelaide, 16 May 2006.

Chapter 4

1. *Prime Minister John Howard's address to the National Press Club on January 25, 2006*, < http://theage.com.au/news/national/pms-speech/2006/01/25/1138066849045.html?page=fullpage contentSwap1>.
2. Janet Albrechtsen, 'Textbook case of making our past a blame game', *The Australian*, 1 February 2006; Kevin Donnelly, 'Why our greatest story is just not being told', *The Australian*, 28 January 2006.
3. Grattan Wheaton, 'Letter', Adelaide *Advertiser*, 27 January 2006; Anne-Marie Irwin, 'Letter', *The Australian*, 27 January 2006.
4. Interview with students, independent Islamic school, Sydney, 23 August 2006.
5. Editorial, 'Canada's history is being lost', *Edmonton Journal*, 2 July 1997; Dan Gardner, 'Canada's lost history', *Ottawa Citizen*, 2 July 1997; JL Granatstein, *Who Killed Canadian History?* (Toronto, HarperCollins, 1998); Rudyard Griffiths, 'Dive back into history', *The Globe and Mail*, 19 October 2001; Dominion Institute, *The Canada Day Youth History Survey* (Angus Reid & The Dominion Institute, 30 June 1997), <http://www.angusreid.com/media/dsp_displaypr_cdn.cfm?id_to_view=871>; Liz Lightfoot, 'Children who think Hitler was British', *Daily Telegraph*, 10 January 2001; Diane Ravitch & Chester E Finn Jnr, *What Do Our 17-Year-Olds Know? A Report on the First National Assessment of History and Literature* (New York, Harper & Row, 1987), p. 201.
6. Sam Wineburg, *Historical Thinking and Other Unnatural Acts: Charting the Future of Teaching the Past* (Philadelphia, Temple University Press, 2001), pp. 306–07.
7. Miranda Kelly, 'Letter', *The Australian*, 19 August 2006.
8. Interview with students, public high school, Northern Territory (near Darwin), 22 June 2006.
9. 'Alex', public high school, Adelaide, 13 June 2006.
10. 'Satisfactory Completion of VCE Units (2006)' Victorian Curriculum and Assessment Authority (2006) <http://www.vcaa.vic.edu.au/vce/statistics/2006/statssect2.html>.
11. John Howard, 'Standard bearer in the fight for liberal culture', *The Australian*, 4 October 2006.
12. The participants at the summit were: Andrew Barnett, Geoffrey Blainey, Geoffrey Bolton, David Boon, Bob Carr, Inga Clendinnen, Kate Darian-Smith, Nick Ewbank, John Gascoigne, Jenny Gregory, Gerard Henderson, John Hirst, Jackie Huggins, Paul Kelly, Jennifer Lawless, Mark Lopez, Gregory Melleuish, Margo Neale, Geoffrey Partington, Lisa Paul, Peter Stanley, Tom Stannage and Tony Taylor.
13. Julie Bishop, 'If we forget our nation's past, we will fail our future', *The Australian*, 17 August 2006.

14 'The Australian History Summit: Transcript of Proceedings' (Canberra, Department of Education, Science and Training, 2006), <http://www.dest.gov.au/NR/rdonlyres/5B7E6762-18E9-4D98-A08E-6BCAA7C1B1DE/13788/history_summit_transcript1.pdf>, p. 1.
15 Julie Bishop, 'Media Release: Australian History Summit' (Canberra, The Hon Julie Bishop MP Media Centre) 18 July 2006, <http://www.dest.gov.au/Ministers/Media/Bishop/2006/07/B001180706.asp>.
16 'The Australian History Summit: Transcript of Proceedings', pp. 8–27.
17 'Margaret', history teacher, public high school, Hobart, 4 May 2006.
18 'Annabel', history teacher, independent high school, Darwin, 21 June 2006; 'Jessica', history teacher, public high school, Brisbane, 25 July 2006.
19 Bob Carr, 'Speech by the Hon. Bob Carr, Premier of NSW, Minister for the Arts, and Minister for Ethnic Affairs, at the 75th Anniversary of the Thirroul Railway Institute, 10 December 1995', *Labour History*, no. 70 (1996), pp. 191, 93; Julie Lewis, 'Carr calls for a return to educational basics', *Sydney Morning Herald*, 6 June 1994.
20 Cited in Kate Cameron, 'The Undermining of History in NSW Schools: A Discussion Paper' (Sydney, History Teachers' Association of New South Wales, 2002), p. 9.
21 Cited in Gerard Noonan, 'Carr's history lesson too boring, teachers say', *Sydney Morning Herald*, 10 October 2002.
22 2002 New South Wales School Certificate results (New South Wales Board of Studies), <http://www.boardofstudies.nsw.edu.au/ebos/static/BDSC_2002_10.htm>; Kathy Lipari, 'Our children know what this Digger did, but not much else', *Daily Telegraph*, 18 December 2002; Cameron, 'The Undermining of History in NSW Schools: A Discussion Paper', p. 4; Noonan, 'Carr's history lesson too boring, teachers say'.
23 'The Australian History Summit: Transcript of Proceedings', p. 17.
24 'Michael', history teacher, public high school, southern New South Wales, 20 July 2006.
25 'Greg', history teacher, independent girls' school, Brisbane, 24 July 2006; 'Jessica', history teacher, public high school, Brisbane, 25 July 2006.
26 Leanne Iselin, Queensland Studies Authority, 26 July 2006.
27 'Neil', history teacher, public senior college, Canberra, 18 August 2006.
28 Interview with students, public high school, Melbourne, 30 March 2006.
29 Interview with students, public high school, New South Wales Central Coast, 22 August 2006.
30 Interview with students, public senior college, Perth, 24 May 2006.
31 'Gail', history teacher, public K–10 school, south-eastern Tasmania, 4 May 2006.

32 'Margaret', history teacher, public high school, Hobart, 4 May 2006.
33 'Greg', history teacher, independent girls' school, Brisbane, 24 July 2006; 'Daniel', history teacher, Catholic boys' school, Brisbane, 25 July 2006; Jan Bishop, former history teacher, Perth, 23 May 2006.
34 Terry Woolley, Executive Director, Primary, Middle and Senior Secondary Services, South Australian Department of Education and Community Services, 15 June 2006.
35 'Sandra', history teacher, public senior college, Perth, 24 May 2006; 'Brian', history teacher, public high school, New South Wales Central Coast, 22 August 2006.
36 Kerry Boyd, Western Australian Curriculum Council, Perth, 22 May 2006.
37 Julie Fisher, Principal Education Officer, Studies of Society and Environment, Tasmanian Department of Education, Hobart, 6 May 2006.
38 Tony Brian-Davis, history teacher and former manager, Commonwealth History Project, 13 June 2006.
39 'Justine', history teacher, public high school, central Australia, 16 June 2006.
40 'Deborah', history teacher, public senior college, Canberra, 18 August 2006; 'Therese', history teacher, selective public school, Sydney, 21 August 2006.
41 'Tahlia', public high school, Melbourne, 16 May 2006.
42 Interview with students, public high school, central Australia, 20 June 2006.
43 Jenny Lawless, Inspector Human Society in Its Environment (including History), New South Wales Board of Studies, 24 August 2006.
44 'Amy', history teacher, independent girls' school, Canberra, 17 August 2006.
45 'Neil', history teacher, public senior college, Canberra, 18 August 2006.

Chapter 5

1 JK Rowling, *Harry Potter and the Philosopher's Stone* (London, Bloomsbury, 1997), p. 9.
2 'Justin', public high school, Perth, 22 May 2006; 'Jiang', independent girls' school, Brisbane, 24 July 2006.
3 'Matilda', independent co-educational school, Adelaide, 13 June 2006; Interview with students, public senior college, Perth, 24 May 2006.
4 'Jamie', public high school, Melbourne, 16 May 2006.
5 Interview with students, public high school, Brisbane, 25 July 2006.
6 'Hanu', independent Islamic school, Sydney, 23 August 2006.
7 'Jade', public senior college, Canberra, 18 August 2006; Interview with

students, public high school, Melbourne, 16 May 2006.
8. 'Allie', independent co-educational school, Hobart, 3 May 2006; 'Yasmin', independent Islamic school, Sydney, 23 August 2006.
9. 'Andie', public girls' high school, Sydney, 21 August 2006; 'John', history teacher, public girls' high school, Sydney, 21 August 2006.
10. Interview with students, public high school, southern New South Wales, 20 July 2006.
11. Interview with students, public senior college, Canberra, 18 August 2006.
12. 'Amy', history teacher, independent girls' school, Canberra, 17 August 2006.
13. 'David', history teacher, public high school, central Australia, 20 June 2006.
14. 'Margaret', history teacher, public high school, Hobart, 4 May 2006.
15. 'Interview with students, independent girls' school, Perth, 24 May 2006; 'Keira', public high school, Northern Territory (near Darwin), 22 June 2006.
16. Interview with students, public K–10 school, south-eastern Tasmania, 4 May 2006.
17. 'Lydia', independent co-educational school, Adelaide, 14 June 2006; 'Andie', public girls' high school, Sydney, 21 August 2006.
18. 'Morgan', independent girls' school, Canberra, 17 August 2006.
19. 'Cameron', history teacher, Catholic boys' school, Perth, 23 May 2006.
20. Interview with students, public high school, Darwin, 21 June 2006; Interview with students, public girls' high school, Sydney, 21 August 2006.
21. 'Ellen', history teacher, public high school, Darwin, 21 June 2006; 'Mary', history teacher, public high school, Brisbane, 26 July 2006; 'Jean', public high school, Melbourne, 30 March 2006.
22. Andrew Metcalfe & Ann Game, *Teachers Who Change Lives* (Melbourne, Melbourne University Press, 2006), chapter 4.
23. 'Sally', history teacher, public P–12 school, central Victoria, 6 May 2006; 'Cameron', history teacher, Catholic boys' school, Perth, 23 May 2006.
24. Tony Taylor, 'Future of the Past – Final Report of the National Inquiry into School History' (Canberra, Department of Education, Training and Youth Affairs, 2000), <http://www.dest.gov.au/sectors/school_education/publications_resources/national_inquiry_into_school_history/the_future_of_the_past_final_report.htm>, chapter 8; Alice Russell, 'In short supply', *The Age*, 30 May 2001.
25. 'Marco', history teacher, public high school, outer Melbourne, 16 May 2006.
26. 'Marco', history teacher, public high school, outer Melbourne, 16 May 2006.
27. 'Deborah', history teacher, public senior college, Canberra, 18 August 2006.

28 'Neil', history teacher, public senior college, Canberra, 18 August.
29 Interview with students, public K–10 school, south-eastern Tasmania, 4 May 2006.
30 Interview with students, independent girls' school, Brisbane, 24 July 2006.
31 Jenny Lawless, Inspector Human Society in Its Environment (including History), New South Wales Board of Studies, 24 August 2006.
32 'Lara', history teacher, public high school, Adelaide, 13 June 2006; 'Greg', history teacher, independent girls' school, Brisbane, 24 July 2006.
33 John McIntyre, Australian Capital Territory Department of Education and Training, 17 August 2006.
34 'The Future of Schooling in Australia' (Melbourne, Council for the Australian Federation, 2007), <http://www.dpc.vic.gov.au/CA256D800027B102/Lookup/FederalistPaper2TheFutureofSchoolinginAustralia/$file/Federalist%20Paper%202%20The%20Future%20of%20Schooling%20in%20Australia.pdf>, pp. 23, 30; Justine Ferrari, 'Diehard subjects return to schools', *The Australian*, 24 April 2007.
35 'Gail', public K–10 school, south-eastern Tasmania, 4 May 2006; 'Jean', public high school, Melbourne, 30 March 2006.
36 'John', history teacher, public girls' high school, Sydney, 21 August 2006; 'Deborah', history teacher, public senior college, Canberra, 18 August 2006.
37 'Stephen', history teacher, Catholic boys' school, Adelaide, 15 June 2006; 'Neil', history teacher, public senior college, Canberra, 18 August.
38 'Brian', history teacher, public high school, New South Wales Central Coast, 22 August 2006.
39 'Jessica', history teacher, public high school, Brisbane, 25 July 2006.
40 John Gore, Chief Education Officer, Human Society in Its Environment, New South Wales Department of Education and Training, 22 August 2006; John Firth, Chief Executive Officer, Victorian Curriculum and Assessment Authority, 13 May 2006.
41 Peter Lee, 'Understanding History' (paper presented at the Canadian Historical Consciousness in an International Context: Theoretical Frameworks conference, University of British Columbia, Vancouver, BC, 2001), <http://www.cshc.ubc.ca/pwias/viewabstract.php?10>. See also: Peter Lee & Rosalyn Ashby, 'Progression of Historical Understanding among Students Ages 7–14', in *Knowing, Teaching and Learning History: National and International Perspectives*, ed. Peter N. Stearns, Peter Seixas & Sam Wineburg (New York & London, New York University Press, 2000), pp. 199–222.
42 Peter Seixas, 'Introduction', in *Theorizing Historical Consciousness*, ed. Peter Seixas (Toronto, University of Toronto Press, 2006), pp.

3–24; Peter Seixas, 'The Purposes of Teaching Canadian History', *Canadian Social Studies* 36, no. 2 (2002), <http://www.quasar.ualberta.ca/css/Css_36_2/Arpurposes_teaching_canadian_history.htm>; Peter Seixas, 'What is Historical Cosnciousness', in *To the Past: History Education, Public Memory, and Citizenship in Canada*, ed. Ruth Sandwell (Toronto, University of Toronto Press, 2006), pp. 11–22; Sam Wineburg, *Historical Thinking and Other Unnatural Acts: Charting the Future of Teaching the Past* (Philadelphia, Temple University Press, 2001); Tony Taylor & Carmel Young, 'Making History: A Guide for the Teaching and Learning of History in Australian Schools' (Canberra, Department of Education, Science and Training, 2003), <http://www.hyperhistory.org/index.php?option=displaypage&Itemid=630&op=page>, p. 15.

43 Jenny Lawless, Inspector Human Society in Its Environment (including History), New South Wales Board of Studies, 24 August 2006; Pat Hincks, Humanities Curriculum Manager, Victorian Curriculum and Assessment Authority, 12 April 2006.
44 'Mary', history teacher, public high school, Brisbane, 26 July 2006.
45 'Daniel', history teacher, Catholic boys' school, Brisbane, 25 July 2006; 'Stephen', history teacher, Catholic boys' school, Adelaide, 15 June 2006.
46 Interview with students, public high school, Darwin, 21 June 2006.
47 Interview with students, public high school, Brisbane, 26 July 2006.
48 'Roger', public high school, Hobart, 4 May 2006; Interview with students, public high school, Perth, 22 May 2006.
49 'Zoran', public senior college, Canberra, 18 August 2006; Interview with students, public high school, Melbourne, 30 March 2006.
50 'Les', public high school, New South Wales Central Coast, 22 August 2006.
51 Interview with students, independent co-educational school, Hobart, 3 May 2006.

Conclusion

1 'Morgan', independent girls' school, Canberra, 17 August 2006; 'Kate', public girls' high school, Sydney, 21 August 2006.
2 'Amy', history teacher, independent girls' school, Canberra, 17 August 2006; 'John', history teacher, public girls' high school, Sydney, 21 August 2006.
3 'Rick', public senior college, Canberra, 18 August 2006.
4 'Ryan', public high school, New South Wales Central Coast, 22 August 2006; 'Martin', Catholic boys' school, Perth, 23 May 2006.
5 'Brian', history teacher, public high school, New South Wales Central Coast, 22 August 2006

6 Paul van Campenhout, Australian Capital Territory Department of Education and Training, 17 August 2006.
7 'Lily', independent girls' school, Brisbane, 24 July 2006.
8 'Felicity', independent girls' school, Canberra, 17 August 2006; 'Lily', independent girls' school, Brisbane, 24 July 2006; 'Jeff', Catholic boys' school, Brisbane, 25 July 2006.
9 'Chen', public girls' high school, Sydney, 21 August 2006; 'Alana', public high school, Perth, 22 May 2006.

Index

Aboriginal history *see* Indigenous history
ABC *see* Australian Broadcasting Corporation
Adelaide Declaration on National Goals for Schooling in the Twenty-first Century (1999), 129
　see also Studies of Society and Environment (SOSE)
Albrechtsen, Janet, 90
America *see* United States
ANOP (polling company), 22
Anzac Day, 3, 47–51, 58, 93
　see also Australians at war
'Anzac Legend' *see* Australians at war
Ashton, Paul, 48
Australia Day, 2–3, 6, 35, 48, 90, 95
Australian Broadcasting Corporation (ABC), 6, 52, 55
　Boyer Lectures, 73
Australian Capital Territory, 10
　Department of Education and Training, 129, 144
　history curriculum, 125, 129
Australian Electoral Commission, 105
Australian identity *see* national values, national identity
Australian Research Council, 7
Australian War Memorial, 36, 48
Australians at war
　'Anzac Legend', 37, 47–48, 57–63
　attitudes towards 'mateship', 46–47, 51, 55, 59
　conscription, 44, 62, 105
　fall of Singapore, 48
　Gallipoli, 24, 45–49, 53, 56, 59, 61
　girls' attitudes to war, 46–47
　protest movement, 44–45
　student prizes, 44, 49
　teaching resources, 49
　Unknown Soldier, 48
　Vietnam War, 105
　Western Front, 24, 45–46, 49
　World War I, 36, 43, 46, 56, 59–61, 105
　World War II, 36, 46, 59, 92, 105

Barton, Edmund, 2, 6, 23–24, 27,

29, 31, 37–38, 41, 42, 94
Barton, Keith, 18
Beare, Julie, 23
bicentenary (1988), 3-4
Bishop, Jan, 62, 103
Bishop, Julie, 35–36, 95
'black armband', 70, 71
    see also 'history wars'
Boston, Ken, 22
Boyd, Kerry, 105–106
Boyer Lectures see Australian
    Broadcasting Corporation
Brett, Judith, 18, 71
Brian-Davis, Tony, 37, 106–107
Britain, 2, 36, 43, 92

Cameron, Kate, 98
Cameron, Rod, 22
van Campenhout, Paul, 144
Canada, 7, 8, 92, 134
Carr, Bob, 97–98
Chifley, Ben, 108
China, 1, 93
civics and citizenship education,
    2, 22–23, 26–27, 42, 97,
    105–106
    Civics Expert Group, 22, 25
    see also federation
Commonwealth History Project,
    26, 37, 106–107
Coniston massacre, 82
    see also Indigenous history
convicts, 36, 104, 70, 104, 105,
    106, 113
    see also First Fleet
Cook, James, 36
curriculum development
    differences between states and
        territories, 4–6, 129–131
    national history curriculum,
        89–111
    need for curriculum
        coordination, 32–33, 68,
        77–78, 88, 104–105, 141
Curtin, John, 109

Daily Telegraph (newspaper,
    Britain), 92

Department of Education, Science
    and Training (DEST), 27
Department of Employment,
    Education, Training and
    Youth Affairs (DEETYA), 27
Department of Veterans' Affairs, 49
Dismissal (1975), 108
Dominion Institute, 92
    see also Canada
Donnelly, Kevin, 90

federation, 20–42
    centenary of federation, 22, 25,
        26–27, 29, 32, 37
        National Council for the
            Centenary of Federation,
            22–23, 26
    repetition of topic in schools,
        33–34, 141
    teaching resources, 26–27
    see also civics and citizenship
        education
feminism see women's history
Finn, Chester E., 92
First Fleet, 3, 36, 106
Firth, John, 48, 133
Fisher, Julie, 73–74, 106
Fitzgerald, Ross, 23

Game, Ann, 123
geography teaching, 12, 23, 90,
    102, 125, 128
Germany, 37
Giles, Janine, 60
goldrushes, 105, 113, 141
Gore, John, 133

Hamilton, Paula, 48
Hawke, Bob, 4, 48
Hincks, Pat, 134–135
history method see history teaching,
    teacher training
history teaching, 112–139
    excursions, 105-6, 116–117
    'historical literacy', 134–135,
        142
    History Teachers' Associations,
        6, 11–12, 49, 73

of Australia, 49
of New South Wales, 98
of Victoria, 124
of Western Australia, 62
primary teaching, 9, 18, 32–33,
    46, 59, 66–68, 75, 78–79,
    89, 126–127, 143
professional development, 12,
    81, 88, 104
rote learning, 113–115
secondary teaching, 9, 11, 32,
    68, 75, 79, 95, 126, 143
teacher training, 12, 123–131
teaching resources, 4, 10, 27–28,
    42, 49, 69, 81, 88, 104,
    107, 117–119, 133, 143
textbooks, 81, 93, 113–116,
    118–119, 131, 136, 137
see also Studies of Society and
    Environment (SOSE)
see also surveys
'history wars', 2, 4–6, 87, 93
Hitler, Adolf, 92
Hobart Declaration on Schooling
    (1989), 129
see also Studies of Society and
    Environment (SOSE)
Hollingworth, Jacqualine, 124
Holocaust, 93
Howard, John, 2, 26, 35, 48,
    51–52, 53, 55, 71, 90–91,
    94–95, 103, 109
    Sir Robert Menzies Lecture
        (1996), 71
    2006 Australia Day address
        (2006), 2, 35, 90, 95

Ihram, Silma, 55
Indigenous history, 3, 11, 14, 30,
    64–88, 104–105
    colonial violence, 4, 82
    feelings of 'guilt', 70–72, 82–3
    historiography, 4, 72–5
    inclusion in curriculum, 72–5
    Indigenous students, 3, 31, 69,
        82–83, 110
    Indigenous teachers, 74–75, 81,
        85

'invasion', 4, 70, 82, 85, 86
reconciliation, 65, 81, 84
repetition of topic in schools, 14,
    66–69, 77–80, 85, 87–88,
    115, 141
Stolen Generations, 75, 93
teaching resources, 81
see also 'history wars'
interviews
    analysis of, 17–18
    process of, 8–13
Irwin, Anne-Marie, 90
Iselin, Leanne, 99–100

Japan, 44, 93

Keating, Paul, 25, 48,
Kirkpatrick, John Simpson, 50, 51,
    54–55, 57

Lawless, Jenny, 4, 110, 128, 134
Levstik, Linda, 18
London terrorist bombings (July
    2005), 53

McGauran, Peter, 52
McIntyre, John, 129
Macintyre, Stuart, 7, 22
Menzies, Robert Gordon, 109
Metcalfe, Andrew, 123
Moran, Anthony, 18
Myall Creek massacre, 82
    see also Indigenous history

National History Summit (August
    2006), 77, 95–98, 100, 103,
    110, 111, 130
    see also curriculum development
National Inquiry into School
    History, 12, 26, 124
National Museum of Australia, 4
National Press Club, 2
national values
    Australian flag, 50, 52–53, 55
    National Framework for Values
        Education, 52–53, 55
    national identity, 3, 25, 43, 44,
        46, 48, 50–51, 53, 55–61,

62–63, 90–91
Nelson, Brendan, 52–55
New South Wales, 4, 5, 10, 73, 77–78, 105, 129
    Department of Education and Training, 133
    history curriculum, 73, 97–99
    History Extension (Higher School Certificate), 87
    mandatory Australian history syllabus, 33, 97–99, 105, 108, 116–117, 133
    New South Wales Board of Studies, 4, 97, 110, 128, 134
    see also history teaching, History Teachers' Associations
Noori, Sarah, 44
Northern Territory, 10, 11
    history curriculum, 125-126

Parkes, Henry, 21
Parliament and Civics Education Rebate, 106
    see also civics and citizenship education
Parliament House, Canberra, 105–106
Pascoe, Susan, 22
Patel, Iqbal, 55
Phillip, Governor Arthur, 3–4
Pinkney, Matthew, 53
Portus, GV, 75
Price, Polly, 53
Print, Murray, 22
private schools see schools
psychology, 94
public schools see schools

qualitative research, 17–18, 65
Queensland, 4, 5, 10, 46, 78, 99, 105
    history curriculum, 78–79, 125, 128-129, 130
    Queensland Studies Authority, 99–100

Ravitch, Diane, 92

Remembrance Day, 3
Returned Services League (RSL), 3
Reynolds, Henry, 74
RSL see Returned Services League

Scates, Bruce, 46
schools
    government, 10, 130, 52, 66, 117–120
    non-government, 10, 11, 118–120, 130
    schools visited, 7–13
    see also history teaching
Simpson and his Donkey see Kirkpatrick, John Simpson
Singapore, 44, 48
SOSE see Studies of Society and Environment
South Australia, 10, 11
    Australian Studies, 68
    Department of Education and Children's Services, 75, 103
    history curriculum, 78, 125
Stanley, Peter, 36
Stanner, WEH, 73
Studies of Society and Environment (SOSE), 5, 12, 78, 106, 125–131
    see also history teaching
surveys, 2, 8, 13, 22–23, 25–26, 42, 91–92

Tasmania, 9, 10, 11
    Department of Education, 73–74, 106
    history curriculum, 125, 130
Taylor, Tony, 7, 12, 24, 96, 124, 134
The Age (newspaper), 44
The Australian (newspaper), 90–91

United States, 18, 23, 24, 69, 92, 109, 134
United Kingdom see Britain

VCAA see Victorian Curriculum and Assessment Authority
Victoria, 3, 4, 10, 44, 49

history enrolments (2006), 94
history curriculum, 125
  see also history teaching, History Teachers' Associations
Victorian Curriculum and Assessment Authority (VCAA), 48, 125, 133–135
Vietnam, 44
  see also Australians at War, the Vietnam War

war history see Australians at war
Western Australia, 10, 11, 105–106

Curriculum Council, 60, 105
history curriculum, 125–126
  see also history teaching, History Teachers' Associations
Wheaton, Grattan, 90
Wilson, Adrian, 53
Wilson, Neil, 3
Windschuttle, Keith, 4
Wineburg, Sam, 92, 134
women's history, 44–45, 73, 83–84, 93, 105
Woolley, Terry, 75, 103

Young, Carmel, 7, 134